sailing passion

coastlines s

es friends laugh

ting drinks sun

sailing passion

coastlines sand

es friends laugh

ting drinks sun

"I dream of things that never were and say why not"

George Bernard Shaw

food wine sun

sailing passion

journeys shore

coastlines sand

water shorelines

friends laugh

eating sailing

eating drinks

Published by Maro 2004
2/3 Brooke Street, Hobart, Tasmania, Australia
Tel : + 61 3 6224 2966
Email : maro@keypoint.com.au
Web: www.maro.com.au

Design & Layout © Julia Dineen
Printed in China by Everbest

ISBN: 0-646-43561-2

Front Cover Image: Fitzroy Island, R Peterswald

contents

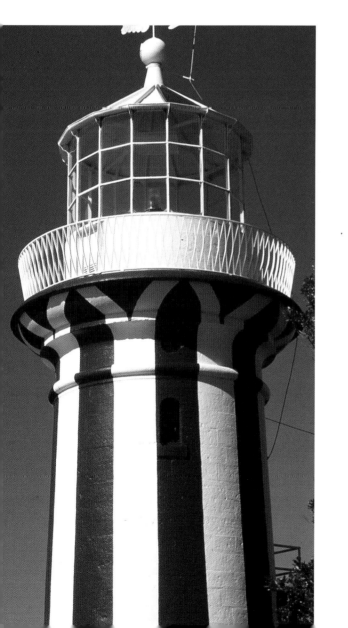

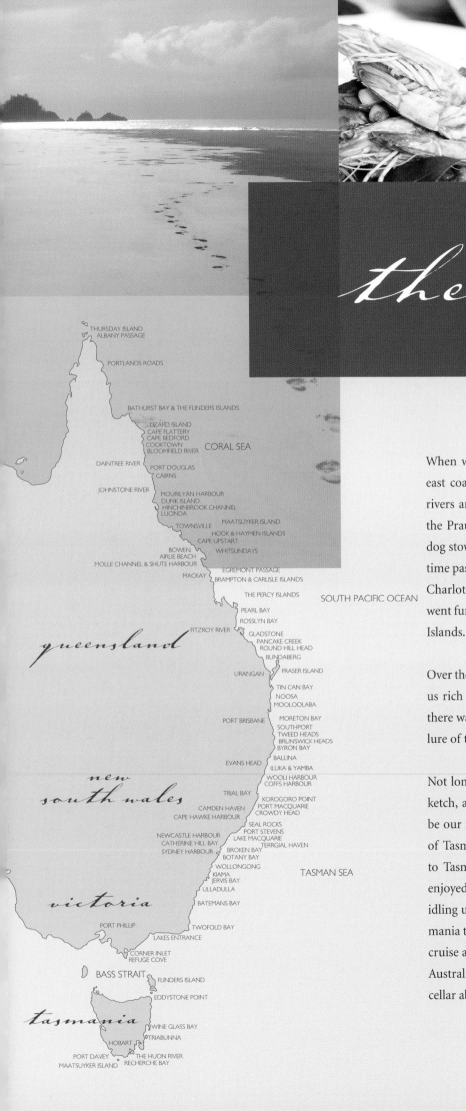

the beginning

When we were young we spent our summers surfing the breaks along the east coast of Australia and mucking around in sailboats and canoes in the rivers and estuaries. Later, after we were married, we bought a small yacht, the Prauwin, and with our two daughters, Charlotte and Georgina and the dog stowed aboard we began to explore the coastline of New South Wales. As time passed and our means permitted we managed to acquire larger craft - the Charlotte Rose, Reveille and Tasman Isle were all much loved yachts - and we went further afield sailing in the waters around Tasmania and the Whitsunday Islands.

Over the years we have had countless wonderful times afloat and we carry with us rich memories that will be with us always. However during all the years there was always something, normally work, to drag us back ashore when the lure of the distant horizon was at its strongest.

Not long ago we acquired Oceania, a beautiful 52' William Garden designed ketch, and decided that in regards to sailing at least, time would no longer be our master. Following this new resolve we embarked on a leisurely cruise of Tasmania, resulting in the publication of 'From the Sea' a book devoted to Tasmania's beautiful sailing waters and fine seafoods and wine. Having enjoyed all that went into creating the book we decided to spend two years idling up the east coast, from the bottom to the top, from Port Davey in Tasmania to Thursday Island in Queensland. 'Beyond the Shore' is a record of the cruise and also touches on fine seafood and wines, provided both by some of Australia's leading restaurants and from the much more humble galley and cellar aboard Oceania.

tasmania

Maatsuyker Island, surrounded by dangerous reefs and battered by the 'roaring forties' lies a few miles off Tasmania's rugged south coast. It was named by the great Dutch navigator Abel Tasman in 1642.

Bramble Cove and Waterfall Bay lie peacefully inside the entrance to Bathurst Channel, and are protected by Breaksea Island while the wind streaked clouds promise a rising gale.

PORT DAVEY TO HOBART

Port Davey and Bathurst Harbour, linked by the fjord like Bathurst Channel, are among Australia's great cruising destinations. Situated on the remote southwest coast of Tasmania they are bounded by the cold vast expanse of the Southern Ocean and the scarcely trodden wilderness of the South West National Park. The surrounding mountains, covered in snow in winter and buffeted by the 'roaring forties' run right down to the cool waters and form dozens of snug anchorages where even the wildest storms can be ridden out in safety. Oceania had been sheltering in one of these, Schooner Cove, for some days waiting for a westerly gale to blow itself out. On board were ourselves, our daughter Charlotte and husband Stephen, their eldest son Hubert and the yet to be born Rufus. When the weather finally broke we headed out in the grey half-light before dawn, bound for Thursday Island at the top of Australia and all ports in between. Once we cleared the Breaksea Islands guarding the entrance to Bathurst Channel we found there was still a large sea running and the reach down to Southwest Cape in a moderate westerly was uncomfortable and cold. Off our port bow the high mountains of the southwest wilderness were hidden behind heaped clouds and apart from the occasional wandering albatross there was no sign of life on the grey heaving sea.

Mount Misery stands sentinel over the entrance to Bathurst Channel.

Standing well clear to avoid a shelving bottom closer in we set a course to pass inside Maatsuyker Islands. These rocky outcrops a few miles off the south coast often shelter a number of lobster boats in the small rocky coves that are the most southerly anchorages of the Australian coast and on the day we passed a number tossed and rolled, only partially protected from the large swell. Occasionally the sun broke through and the beauty of the southern mountains, range after range of misty blue, was revealed. Then the wind would chase another rain squall onto us and we would spend a few uncomfortable minutes until it had passed. By mid afternoon we were off South East Cape, both the southern most part of the coast and the longitude at which we passed into the Pacific Ocean, and had begun to swing northward on the journey to the top of Australia. Shortly afterwards, beyond Whale Point, we found shelter from the great westerly rollers that sweep across the bottom of Tasmania having run unchecked half way around the world. Off Recherche Bay, named after the ship of Admiral Bruni d'Entrecasteaux who anchored there in 1792, we navigated carefully through the reef-strewn Acteon Islands and in the last of daylight edged into the small fishing port of Dover where we dropped anchor off the jetty, protected by the islands, Faith, Hope and Charity.

Port Davey the Connemara of Tasmania

The next day our younger daughter Georgie joined us, while Cha, Hubie and Stephen returned to Hobart after having spent a week aboard. The skies had cleared overnight and with the wind still fresh from the southwest we had a great run across the estuary of the Huon River. For most of last century the Huon river was as famous for its apples as it was for the beautiful timber that bears its name and it is from here that many of the apples used to make Tasmanian ciders are still grown. More recently a number of picturesque vineyards, which are the most southern in Australia, have been established along the green and rolling valley, studded also with stands of tall timber and old Federation cottages. Past the Huon River the D'Entrecasteaux Channel, a beautiful stretch of water that lies between Bruny Island and the mainland, continues northward. On both shores green-forested slopes, broken in places by patches of cleared farmland and small hamlets, run down to the waters edge. As we sailed past the Channel was dotted with sails gleaming in the sunshine while in the many protected coves boats of all shapes and sizes were snugly anchored. These clean cool waters produce some of Australia's finest Atlantic salmon, fattening in large netted pens suspended in the water by rows of black buoys. After an exhilarating sail we anchored overnight off the small village of Kettering, and enjoyed the late afternoon sun before it finally slipped behind the ranges. Later we rowed ashore and dined on chilled Pacific Oysters with a pint of Cascade stout in the gardens of the Kettering Hotel, a favourite haunt of ours, set in beautiful grounds overlooking the Oyster Cove Marina.

We awoke to a morning of complete calm, the channel around us untroubled by any whisper of breeze or hint of wash. In the early golden light the still water was a mirror holding perfect reflections of the colourful yachts and launches, the jetties on the southern shore, the steeply forested point and the gulls that floated motionlessly behind our stern. We idled the morning away, waiting for the arrival of the afternoon's sea breeze to carry us up the Derwent to Hobart. Shortly, after a simple lunch on the quarterdeck, the approaching wind was heralded by the advance of ruffled water up the channel and we weighed anchor and hoisted all sail. The run up the Derwent, one of the worlds great harbours, on a summer's warm sea breeze is always a noble experience. Past the old pilot station and the rocky foreshore at Tinderbox the breeze freshens and carries with it the smell of the open sea as flecks of cooling spray are thrown up from the swells surging beneath the rollicking stern. Ahead the rivers wide expanse opens to distant views of the city and high blue mass of Mount Wellington framed by a pale cerulean sky. As we drew closer the broad estuary became a kaleidoscope of colour: the red and white of flitting sails, the cream of churning wakes, brilliant ballooning

ABALONE

Tasmanian waters, particularly on the west and south coasts yield the finest abalone in the world. Unfortunately nearly all the commercial catch is exported, mostly to Japan where it is a particularly cherished delicacy. Generally if you wish to eat abalone you must be prepared to dive for it yourself or have a generous friend do it for you. Even so, the catch is strictly regulated and a license is required.

Most commonly in Tasmania Abalone is cut into thin slices about 2 mm thick, gently tenderized with a wooden mallet and fried or barbecued for perhaps 30 seconds (until the flesh changes from translucent to white, but be careful not to overcook). Many marinate before cooking either in a white wine, lemon or the juices of the fish and it can be served with a variety of garnishes including teriyaki, soy, garlic and lemon. It can be tossed through a salad and/or served on a bed of noodles.

An alternative method of cooking, and one that would have been preferred by Admiral Bruni D'Entrecasteaux and his sailors, the first to anchor in Recherche Bay, and who would have enjoyed abalone (known as ormers) in the Channel Ports, would have been to bake them. The whole abalone is cooked for 4-5 hours (depending on the size) in olive oil in a covered dish at 110c and carved into thin slices when cool. A number of herbs or spices can be placed in the olive oil (but be careful not to overpower) including; garlic, fennel, cinnamon or perhaps a dash of Vermouth or Pernod.

An old gaff rigged ketch anchored near Cockle Creek in Recherche Bay, the most southern anchorage on Tasmania's east coast.

TASMANIAN CIDERS

When Captain Cook planted an apple tree at Adventure Bay on Bruny Island in 1777 it was the first recorded European fruit introduced into Australia. After Hobart was founded in 1803 it was not long before orchards were planted in what are now the city's central suburbs and as the colonists pushed into the wilderness they took with them many of the old traditional English varieties of apples and pears to form the basis of their homestead orchards. Many of these early settlers had come from the south of England where cider making was an ancient ritual and as the orchards were maturing rough crushers and presses were made from whatever was at hand. Some presses were even large sandstone wheels turned by harnessed horses, but in the most part they were simple rack and cloth affairs, or slatted basket presses, and the juice was fermented naturally in wooden barrels and drunk fresh and rough.

SUSHI OF ATLANTIC SALMON, AVOCADO AND SCALLOPS

Make a sauce of rice vinegar, sugar and salt.

Mix with rice and leave aside for two hours.

Place rice on seaweed and add salmon, avocado, egg and scallops, mixed with Japanese mayonnaise sauce. Roll with ingredients in centre. Cut into size and eat with extra mayonnaise sauce or if you prefer soya and wasabi, however Mikaku tells us the traditional way is with Japanese mayonaise.

Mikaku restaurant is popular with many tourists and locals and is situated right in the heart of Salamanca Place amidst historic sandstone buildings.

Toss about 60gm whitebait per person in seasoned flour.

Make an aioli by whisking 3 free range egg yolks, garlic and vinegar together. Slowly add saffron oil (made from 3 fronds saffron soaked in 400 ml olive oil overnight) which should be a rich yellow. Whisk oil in a slow steady stream until the mix thickens. Season with salt and pepper.

Heat a deep pot of vegetable oil until very hot and fry whitebait for a few seconds until golden brown.

Serve on Rocket leaves (dressed with cider vinegar and extra virgin olive oil) add lemon wedges and a generous dollop of the aioli on the side.

Amy Currant suggests accompanying this dish with a Tassie Riesling from Apsley Gorge Vineyard or another wine with a sharp acid contrast.

PEPPERMINT BAY

WHITEBAIT

Peppermint Bay is another of well known Tasmanian, Simon Currant's wonderful additions to the Tasmanian tourist experience. Set on the shores of the D'Entrecasteaux Channel the stunning restaurant, with it's award winning design, is ideally arrived at by the Peppermint Bay catamaran which hugs the coastline from Hobart to Woodbridge, or otherwise one can meander down picturesque byways by car, stopping at small villages along the way. Simon is well known for his previous icons in Tasmania, including Cradle Mountain Lodge and Strahan Village, both worthy of a visit.

Hobart nestles below the great bulk of Mount Wellington

spinnakers, the square rigged canvas of the Lady Nelson, all framed by the enveloping ridges running high beyond each shore. The Hobart docks, lined by sandstone buildings of early colonial times, retain much of the charm of the age of tall rigged ships. In summer it is the destination of many who come here by sail. Some aboard the sleek and powerful yachts of the Sydney – Hobart race fleet, others in much loved wooden boats created from local huon or celery pine, or perhaps of cedar, oak or mahogany for the Wooden Boats Festival. Others aboard cruising yachts of every shape

The Ruby Charlotte, once from the Percy Islands, visiting Hobart.

and size, some travelled stained and weary, others with shining bright work and polished hulls. On the bustling dock side, alive with music and laughter, the mariners are lost among the throng eddying here and there amidst the crowded bars and laden tables, the buskers and bands, or lying in the deep shade of the ancient oaks. It is these that mark the approach of winter and in the golden glow of autumn their leaves, kissed by the sun and blushing reds and gold, drop gently to the cooler lawns. In winter, when the southerly gales heap snow on the slopes of Mount Wellington and

CHAR GRILLED OCTOPUS

Plunge 700gm Octopus legs (peeled) into boiling water for 4-5 minutes. Drain then cool in iced water to stop the cooking process. Marinate in 200ml olive oil, 4 cloves garlic and 1 tablespoon ground black pepper and one lemon sliced, then set aside.

Cut 2 large zucchinis, 1 large red onion, 2 red peppers, 200gm baby spinach leaves into even size pieces and char grill for 1-2 minutes on each side, set aside. Whisk together 200 ml olive oil, 150ml red wine vinegar, 1/2 bunch of chopped dill and salt and pepper to taste, drizzle over vegetables and let marinate for at least 1 hour.

To assemble dish, char grill octopus and lemon halves for 2 minutes on each side then stack vegetables, octopus and spinach on a plate and drizzle with extra red wine vinaigrette and squeezed char grilled lemon.

OVEN ROASTED WHOLE SNAPPER WITH GREEK STYLE SALAD AND FRESH LIME.

Pre heat oven to 220c. Whisk together juice of 2 lemons, 50gm freshly chopped oregano leaves, 150ml olive oil and 2 cloves garlic. Place 4 whole fish, cleaned and gutted on oven tray, lined with silicon paper and drizzle with lemon and oregano mixture, then season with salt and pepper. Roast fish for 10-12 minutes or until firm to the touch.

Mix all the salad ingredients, (mixed lettuce leaves, 100gm semi-dried tomatoes, ½ red onion, 1 small Lebanese cucumber, 150gm good quality Greek fetta, 150gm whole kalamata olives, 1 lime quartered) drizzle with salad dressing (150ml olive oil, 50ml white wine vinegar, 50gm freshly chopped oregano leaves) and then serve with whole fish with lime wedges.

Serves 4

Athenas has a double frontage to the Hobart Docks with fishing boats and million dollar yachts tied up alongside. It is one of our favourite local restaurants serving traditional Greek dishes and local seafood with a Mediterranean flavour.

ATHENAS

ON THE DOCKS

Over summer the Hobart waterfront dances to a different beat as the Sydney-Hobart yacht race finishes and the Taste of Tasmania and the Wooden Boats Festival get into full swing.

PAN SEARED FISH WITH VINE ROASTED TOMATOES & TAPENADE

200gm of cleaned fish fillets per person.

To make the tapenade: blend with mortar and pestle 100gm pitted kalamata olives, 3 peeled cloves garlic and 5 anchovy fillets with a little olive oil to make a thick paste.

Wash 6-8 small tomatoes still attached to the vine per person and let dry. Heat a small amount of virgin olive oil in a large pan until smoking. Season the fish then sear it until you see a golden tinge on the edge and turn over. Add the tomatoes and garlic and place in a pan in the oven and cook till tender.

Arrange fresh picked herbs, such as flat leaf parsley, tarragon, thyme, basil, sage and oregano around the plate with splodges of the tapenade. Place the fish in the centre and lay the tomatoes over the fish. Drizzle with olive oil and serve.

Serves 4.

Accompany with a Chardonnay or a light Pinot.

PEPPERMINT BAY

TASMANIAN WINES

The first Tasmanian vineyard was established in Newtown, now a suburb of Hobart, by Captain Swanston in 1823 and wine from these vines won Tasmania's first international award in Paris in 1848. Wine is still produced from the remnants of these ancient vines, as it is also produced from vines planted on Tasmania's east coast by German settlers in the 1830's. However the genesis of Tasmania's modern wine industry was in the 1950's when two visionaries, Jean Miguet near Pipers Brook in the north of the state, and Claudio Alcorso at Moorilla near Hobart proved that the state's climate was ideal for many varieties. The cool climate and long autumn days give the grapes a long ripening, enhancing the elegant flavours and aromas of the wines. There are six distinct regions in the state, each exhibiting unique characteristics, and producing some of the worlds finest rieslings, gewurztraminers, chardonnays and pinot noirs as well as great full bodied reds from the Tamar valley in the north, and legendary sparkling wines from Pipers Brook.

Part of the wooden boat fleet moored before the old Customs House in Constitution Dock, Hobart

the pale sun creeps low on the horizon, the city moves to a slower pace. Warm fires burn behind doors drawn tight against the chill and scarfs are wound beneath cold and rosy cheeks. In the early dark the lights along Salamanca Place shine warm and golden from behind windows set deep in ancient sandstone, the laughter within and the sound of harp and fiddle muted by the deep walls.

The dramatic coastline of Tasman Island and the Tasman Peninsula.

HOBART TO TRIABUNNA

By the time we had motored to Dennes Point, which marks the northern tip of Bruny Island, a breeze was drawing down the Derwent and before long we had enough to fill a steadying sail. There was hardly any swell in Storm Bay and we lounged around the decks enjoying the deep blue of sea and sky as we followed a course for distant Cape Raoul. By mid day the sea breeze had come up and we had an enjoyable run across the great rocky cliff faces from Cape Raoul to Cape Pillar and Tasman Island. Tasman Island is always unforgettable. At dawn on a clear day it can be an enchantress sitting on the horizon, coloured blue and tinged with the roses of dawn. Or it can be wrapped in low storm clouds lashed by wind, the most hostile place on earth with the voices of doomed sailors still echoing off the sheer rock walls of the inside passage. This stretch of coastline is as dramatic as any in Australia, steep high cliff-faces, carved into fantastic patterns by the battering of ages tower above passing boats. We sailed through the narrow channel inside Tasman Island and rounded Pyramid Rock before heading north again. An hour later we had reached the shelter of Fortescue Bay and anchored behind the old wreck in its northern reach. Thick forests completely envelop the bay with giant eucalypts lining the edge, while in the dark waters heavy with seaweed a diver can often be rewarded with a succulent crayfish and abalone or a feast of delicious mussels. With the onset

The sheer walls of Tasman Island dwarf the old flying fox station once used to resupply the lighthouse.

The anchorage at Pirates Bay.

Moorilla Estate, under the direction of Claudio Alcorso, was one of the leaders in the renaissance of the Tasmanian wine industry. It is set on a beautiful peninsula in the Derwent River a few miles north of Hobart where it is overlooked by the often snow capped Mount Wellington and lapped by the ebb and flow of the river. Over the years it has built up an impressive record of national and international awards and produces wines we have always enjoyed. It is a great place to visit - the vineyard is often filled with music and good cheer and a museum of antiquities of international standard is located in the original Roman style villa that Claudio built to enjoy his beautiful surrounds. Along a high bank overlooking the Derwent, perched on tall poles, there are a number of delightful cottages where you can let life and the river flow peacefully past.

GRILLED GARNISHED MUSSELS

Mussels grow naturally all over Tasmania and in nearly any bay they can be collected from the rocks when the tide is out. Mostly they are enjoyed after boiling for a few minutes in wine or water and herbs.

With a little more effort the boiled mussels can be garnished and grilled and made into a fine dish with a French flavour.

Take each boiled mussel half shell with the mussel attached and garnish with herbed butter (garlic, parsley, finely chopped shallot, lemon zest, salt and pepper) topped with bread crumbs and grill for a few minutes until crisp and golden brown. Serve immediately.

'Molly' and three old shipmates at Cascades, Koonya, overlooking Norfolk Bay.

of night it was once again completely still and from the shadows of the trees the laugh of a kingfisher was answered by its mate. There was no sign of man ashore and none, other than the rusting remains of the old wreck, on the water.

During the night a front moved across the state and in the morning fresh south westerlies were tossing the higher branches of the surrounding forest and ruffling the waters of the bay. Keeping a careful eye on the depth sounder we edged out past the old wreck at the bottom of the tide and hoisted the reefed main and staysail. Outside the bay the wind had flattened the sea and staying close in we had a good run up the rocky coastline, still dominated by high bluffs and sheer cliff faces. Lobster boats were setting pots close in while further out fishermen worked the reefs around the Hippolite Rocks. The wind channels across the beach at Pirates Bay and for a while we sailed through fields of dancing white caps before reaching the protection of the high cliffs of the Forestier Peninsula. By early afternoon we were inside Maria Island gliding through the translucent blue waters of the Mercury Passage, so clear that every detail of the sandy bottom seemed close enough to touch and the stingrays idling there lazily eyed our passing. To our right the high peaks of Maria Island were silhouetted against a perfect sky, their heavily wooded slopes running down to the gleaming sands that fringed the beautiful ellipse of Chinaman's Bay. On the mainland the villages of Orford and Triabunna began to emerge from the background. Although the tide was making as we picked our way up the shallow channel into Triabunna we breathed a sigh of relief when we were over the worst and a few moments later had tied up at the wharf under the friendly directions of Stan Berry, the harbour master. This was Georgie's last night on board until we reached Queensland and we all had a tear in our eyes when we waved her off the next day.

SEAFOOD SALAD WITH THAI DRESSING

Allow 50gm each per person of sliced octopus, blue eye (or other firm fish), calamari and whole Tasmanian scallops. Mix together with enough olive oil to coat. Heat large iron frying pan untill very hot. Place all seafood into dry pan, cook for 30 seconds then shake pan to turn seafood once only. Mix hot seafood through some Asian greens with a Thai dressing (50ml lime juice, 50ml water, 25ml fish sauce, 25gm Palm sugar, 4 cloves sliced garlic, 6 sliced Thai chillies, ½ red sliced capsicum, chopped coriander leaves and 100ml olive oil mixed together) and arrange on plate. Serve with some tempura vegetables. A Freycinet Chardonnay is an ideal companion to this wonderful easy dish. Serves 4.

Geoff Copping has been synonymous with fine food in Hobart for many years. Blue Skies is just on our doorstep and quite often we wander down and sit outside in the late twilight to enjoy all that this fine restaurant offers, not least of which is the magnificent setting.

Bream Creek Vineyard overlooks beautiful Marion Bay, with the noble hump of Maria Island in the distance. It is not far from the place where Abel Tasman became the first European explorer to set men ashore on the island that now bears his name, The location, open to the sun and sea enables the grapes to ripen slowly and fully in the long cooler days of summer and early autumn and produces full flavoured wines with a hint of the ocean's tang. The vineyard is known for it's elegant pinot noirs, rieslings, chardonnays, sauvignon blancs and schonburgers and is an excellent place to while away a few hours during an exploration of the Forestier and Tasman Peninsulas, places of great beauty and historical interest.

The rugged mountain ranges of Maria Island off Tasmania's east coast

TRIABUNNA TO EDDYSTONE POINT

Last night the "new" crew came on board. Hardly new though. We have known Sue and Don Clark since we arrived in Tasmania over twenty years ago. They owned the neighbouring farm at Koonya and were, apart from Bruce and Marjorie Heyward whom we had bought our farm from, the first people we met in Tasmania. Peter "Bluey" Knight we knew twenty years before that, when we were teenagers in Canberra. After restocking Oceania with fresh fruit, vegetables and meat from the fields of the Tasman Peninsula and delicious home cooked rock cakes that are one of Sue's specialities we spent the evening at the peaceful Triabunna Jetty rafted alongside a fishing boat. In the long twilight we grilled fresh Atlantic Salmon on the barbecue mounted on the quarterdeck, reminisced and discussed the passage to Sydney. Triabunna, tucked around the protected waters of Spring Bay, is home to a fishing fleet of a dozen or so boats that work the beautiful waters between Pirates Bay on the Tasman Peninsula and Wine Glass Bay to the north.

An autumn vineyard near Swansea on Tasmania's east coast where wine has been grown since early colonial times

We cast off shortly after 8 am when the making tide gave us sufficient depth to comfortably navigate the shallow channel into Spring Bay. Before long we rounded Cape Bougainville and carrying all sail in a light westerly laid a course for Schouten Passage. The early morning cloud soon gave way to warm sunshine and the sparkling sapphire waters danced around us. It is rare to cross Great Oyster Bay without the company of dolphins, and as we passed Ile des Phoques, Cape Faure and entered the beautiful Schouten Passage they came and went, their usual friendly and carefree selves, eager to play in the wash of our bow.

Looking across Great Oyster Bay to The Hazards and Coles Bay.

Only accessible by foot or boat Wine Glass Bay is one of Tasmania's favourite spots. The narrow entrance gives protection in most winds to an anchorage off the long crescent of white beach, and is particularly secure when the wind is from the west. The high granite cliffs wrap around on all sides, their majesty drawing our eyes upward from the changing blues of the bay, the white of the breaks along the shore and the cleanly washed sand of the beach. We shared the anchorage with three other yachts and half a dozen fishermen who very kindly donated a dinner of flathead, which we filleted and poached in wine – delicious. As the last of the sun set behind Wineglass Beach it left a golden glow on the high granite cliffs and the boats strung along the deserted beach.

Wineglass Bay

The gleaming granite bluffs at the entrance to Wineglass Bay on the sea-ward side of the Freycinet Peninsula

After a peaceful night we headed off with the first of the dawn, intent on making Eddystone Point, nearly eighty nautical miles away. Again the wind blew steadily from the west and we reached up the coast with all sail, doing better than seven knots most of the time. With the wind blowing off the shore we stayed close in and enjoyed the beauty of the coastline as it slid past – the high peaks of Ben Lomond National Park, long white beaches and rocky outcrops with the sun playing on the fiery red lichen that is a highlight of this area. We passed Bicheno with its picturesque anchorage in "the Gulch" and in late afternoon the small holiday village of Binalong Bay, sitting on the southern end of the stunning stretch of beaches that line

Bay of Fires.

the Bay of Fires. We anchored just on dusk to be greeted by a friend of Don and Sue bearing a feast of crayfish. This quickly silenced the debate on what to have for dinner, although we had to decide on having them fresh, or mornayed with Rosemary's famous sauce. The Mornay won and it was delicious served with chilled white wine on the aft deck, after an entree of grilled scallops, while the beam of the Eddystone light flashed overhead in the gathering gloom.

Bring juice of 1 lemon to boil. Add touch of sea salt, pepper and 1 teaspoon of sugar. Add 1 tablespoon capers. Slowly add knobs of butter to taste. A small amount of cream can be added at the end if the sauce tastes too buttery.

Preheat grill to hot. Coat four 200gm deep sea trevalla with flour and lemon and pepper, shake off excess. Barbecue fish until just cooked and golden, garnish with lemon butter and serve with fresh steamed snow peas, carrots and asparagus and baked tomatoes. Serves 4.

Acclaimed Australian architect Ken Latona designed and built the Bay of Fires Lodge a number of years ago and ever since it has attracted much admiration both for its stunning location and eco friendliness.

From the sea, as we sailed past to our anchorage under Eddystone Point lighthouse, it is barely visible but commands fine coastal views.

Heath, the long time and well known manager, who cooked this dish for us, when we visited a few months ago, says the food here, apart from being delicious, must be fresh and hearty to satisfy the appetites of the many walkers who arrive from the magnificent Bay of Fires Walk which ambles along the beach and takes in some mesmerizing scenery. To reach the lodge one must do the walk. There is, in fact, no other way of being fed!! But may we assure you it is well worth the walk as was reiterated by the guests we met there, pictured on the right

BAY OF FIRES

BARBECUED
TREVALLA

The remote 'Bay of Fires' on Tasmania's northeast coast is lined by fine white beaches and great granite boulders marked by the sea and striking red lichen. It is a place to escape the world and enjoy the wash of the sea and the breeze in your face. At the northern end an anchorage is the last before Bass Strait.

33

EDDYSTONE POINT TO EDEN

Although the forecast issued by Mersey Radio predicted strong westerlies the morning dawned bright and with winds moderate enough to encourage us into Banks Strait, the notorious stretch of water between the Tasmanian coastline and the Furneaux Group of islands. Here the roaring forties are funneled into a relatively narrow and shallow channel and they can produce murderous seas – particularly if working against the swift tidal race between Cape Portland and Clarke Island. By the time we were abeam of Clarke Island the forecast winds had arrived, gusting to 25 knots. We

OCEAN TROUT WITH LIME & CHILLI

Combine crushed garlic, grated ginger and grated lime rind and brush the fleshy side of trout fillets or cutlets. Heat 50gm of butter and 2 tablespoons of peanut or macadamian nut oil in a pan and cook trout (best medium rare), remove and keep warm. Add to the pan, halves of baby bok choy, sweet chilli sauce, lime juice, and crushed garlic and cook until bok choy is tender. Sprinkle the trout with fresh chopped coriander and serve with rice and bok choy mixture and lime wedges. But this is only one of many ways to cook fresh trout as pictured above.

TASMANIAN BEERS

The early settlers soon realised that the area around Sorrell and Richmond in southern Tasmania, with fertile valleys and warm dry summers was ideal for growing wheat and barley, and before long most of the local needs were grown in this region and the often large surpluses exported to Sydney. There were also ideal hop growing areas in the Huon and Derwent River valleys and a plentiful supply of fresh clean water. Add the ever-growing demand for beer from the expanding colony and all the elements for the growth of a brewing industry were present. These days the traditions of Tasmanian brewing are maintained by The Cascades Brewery in Hobart and Boags in Launceston where beers of international acclaim are produced from the finest local ingredients.

The Bay of Fires Lodge is tucked into the hills above a secluded beach

GRILLED SCALLOPS WITH WALNUT AND CORIANDER GARNISH

Tasmanian scallops are amongst the state's most famous exports and subject to the ravages of man have grown prolifically in sandy seabeds around the state. They are often eaten fried in batter or breadcrumbs or served in their shells with a variety of garnishes and sauces. This dish combines them with walnuts, a tree that came with the early settlers and graces many older gardens in Tasmania.

For one dozen scallops. Fry a tablespoon of crushed walnuts in an oiled pan for 2-3 minutes. Add four tablespoons of butter, a pinch of chopped coriander, parsley, shallot, salt, pepper and a dash of lemon and heat gently for a few minutes. Pre-heat grill. Brush the scallops lightly with the garnish and grill in their shells for 1 minute. Add a teaspoon of garnish to each shell and grill for a further 2 minutes. Serve immediately.

Lobster boat off Eddystone Point

Pipers River, in the north of Tasmania was chosen as a site for vineyards because of the many characteristics it shares with some of France's famous wine growing regions. Here deep alluvial soil and a vigorous cool climate combine to produce still and sparkling wines of world renown. Pipers Brook Vineyard is the best known of the wineries in this area and along with Moorilla in the south were leaders in the reinvigoration of the wine industry. Other wineries close by include, the Bay of Fires, Brook Eden, Clover Hill, Dalrymple, Delamere and Providence Vineyards.

Eddystonee Point lighthouse stands sentinel on the north eastern tip of Tasmania.

reefed the mainsail, only to drop it almost immediately as the gusts continued to build to gale force, and continued under mizzen and staysail. The seas were now most uncomfortable and we were glad to take refuge in Jamieson Bay, a small snug anchorage under the eastern tip of Cape Barren Island. Here we were protected from the southwest through to the northeast and could enjoy the dramatic beauty of the high rocky mountains and rock strewn beach. Without exception the fishermen who work these remote waters are the most considerate and hospitable of people. We were very pleased to see two boats sheltering here – it is always reassuring to know the professionals have chosen the same anchorage. Oceania had only just bedded the anchor when one of the fishermen came to say hello and left us with a huge crayfish. As it was much too big for any pot on board we baked it in the barbecue and later ate it chilled and garnished with a Pernod and olive oil dressing. Beautiful. Meanwhile the wind settled in at a steady thirty-five knots and we let out more chain and prayed it did not back much further south.

The rocky foreshore at Jamieson Bay on Cape Barren Island.

A lobster boat sheltering from a freshening south westerly at Jamieson Bay.

Dawn offered a brief respite from the gale that had blown for two days, although it was forecast to build again in the afternoon. We took the opportunity of moving to Babel Island, some thirty-five miles away. Rounding Cape Barren we waved goodbye to our friends fishing the nearby reefs and rode the tidal current north, staying well out to clear the dangerous shoals around the "Pot Boil". By mid morning the high peak of Babel had emerged from the light blue haze and the "mare's tails" streaking the western sky warned us that the promised winds were not far off. We anchored off the beach below Sellars Point, a good anchorage protected from the west and southwest by the curve of the Flinders Island coast and from the north by Babel Island and the isthmus that connects the two. Shortly afterwards we were glad to be joined by three lobster boats and a couple of trawlers. Once again we were delighted by their consideration. It seems as if most fishermen feel a personal responsibility for boats visiting their remote patch of ocean. As it turned out Sue had taught one of the young men some years before at the Tasman District School, so there were a few exaggerations thrown about and we were once again left to feast on lobster. By dusk the winds had returned and during the night they built to over forty-five knots. We were more than thankful to have sixty metres of heavy chain out and a 120 lb plough anchor firmly dug in.

A windswept anchorage off the beach at Flinders Island with Babel Island to the north..

Late on Wednesday night the wind finally blew itself out. It had blown over forty-five knots for much of the day and the large trawlers on either side of us dragged and had to reset their anchors more than once. After checking the Mersey Radio morning sched on Thursday and down loading a weather fax we decided there was an opportunity to make a run for Eden. At 9 am we cleared Storehouse Island, a small companion off Babel's east coast and laid a course for Eden, some two hundred miles north. The ocean, with a large swell still running and freshly washed by four days of gales was a startling turquoise. The air was crisp and clean, the autumn sun warm on the deck; what more could we ask for? In the late morning we passed a school of small fish herded by dolphins into such a dense mass that for all the world it seemed to be a large submerged shoal. A few well-fed dolphins took some time out to frisk around the boat before returning to their somewhat gruesome duty. Later a beautiful red sunset heralded a fine star filled night, and then in the last of the pre-dawn darkness we caught the loom of Rame Head lighthouse. Shortly afterwards the spire of Gabo lighthouse climbed out of the shining water, silhouetted against the golden orb of the rising sun. A most welcome sight, followed shortly afterwards by a large breakfast of Rosemary's bacon and eggs. At 3 pm we entered picturesque Twofold Bay and tied up to the western jetty of the pretty fishing town of Eden.

LOBSTER

There are many ways of cooking lobsters however this is an easy and failsafe way. Split and clean the lobster (retaining the juices) and place in a preheated oven (180c-190c), or in a covered barbecue and baste with garlic butter until cooked. Serve with garnish.

Garnish: Combine over a low heat: the lobster juices, 100ml olive oil, chopped shallots, parsley, dash of mustard, dash of lemon juice, salt and pepper and a pinch of tarragon to taste, finally add a dash of Pernod (again to taste).

This is one of Georgie and Simon's favourite dishes which we often serve on board Oceania.

With its nineteenth century stone cottage sitting on a small knoll overlooking the rows of gnarled vines and the Swan River ambling gently past, sluggish in the summer heat, Craigie could be a little part of Tuscany. John Austwick came to grow grapes near Swansea on Tasmania's east coast over thirty years ago and his was the first of the latter day vineyards to realise the areas potential. Along with Freycinet, Spring Vale and Coombend vineyards this area produces some great full bodied cabinet sauvignons, aromatic and full flavoured pinot noirs, rieslings, schonbergs, gewurztraminers, pinot gris and chardonnays. The summers are warmer and drier along the east coast, giving the region late fully ripenned fruit bursting with the taste of sunshine and the sea.

Meadowbank is one of Tasmania's signature wineries, with grapes grown in both the higher country of the upper Derwent Valley, where vines have been established for many years and in the rich alluvial soils near the historic town of Richmond. A visit to the Richmond vineyard is an occasion to remember. Fine food and wine are served in a stunning restaurant overlooking the vineyard and the sparkling waters of Pittwater. There is an art gallery and seasonal programs of music, art and food and wine events.

The fishermen working the dangerous waters off Flinders Island are a resilient group, cheerful and hospitable. As are the crew of Oceania in Bass Strait.

Boathouses at Brighton

Toss together the following ingredients for the Japanese salad: tablespoon wakami seaweed, sliced cucumber, sliced bamboo shoots, sliced carrot, bean shoots, blanched beans, blanched spinach, sliced shitake.

Combine the following for the Nam-Jim dressing: 1 crushed garlic clove, 6 coriander stalks, 1 tablespoon sea salt, 4 green chilli, 2 tablespoons palm sugar, 3 tablespoons fish sauce, 6 tablespoon lime juice, 4 sliced shallots.

For the crayfish tortellinis lay 1 wanton skin down, paint with beaten egg, place nori sheet on top and paint, add crayfish mix (julienne snow peas, blanched spinach, red chilli diced, 50gm diced cooked crayfish) and fold into parcels, deep fry for 2-3 minutes.

Panfry Kingfish for 4-5 minutes and serve ontop of the salad and tortellinis. Decorate with cray shells and legs.

BEAUMARIS PAVILION

HIRAMASA KINGFISH WITH CRAYFISH TORTELINIS AND JAPANESE SEAWEED SALAD

The Beaumaris Pavilion has been a landmark on Port Phillip Bay for over a hundred years and although the restaurant has been extensively updated the Pavilion still retains the character that has made it such an integral part of the community over the years. It was such a glorious day when we visited that we carried the table across the road and this is where we photographed Dave and James who prepared this fabulous dish for us.

southern nsw

Alastair, a lone sailor heading north.

EDEN TO BATEMANS BAY.

We had scarcely docked at Eden before fresh northerlies set in and encouraged us to enjoy the port for a few days. Eden holds a special place in most yachtsmen's hearts. Although it is often crowded and berths sometimes hard to come by, it is a safe haven while waiting to cross Bass Strait, or a welcome refuge once the crossing has been made. In either case, the pathos of the crossing adds to the already considerable charms of the town. We had fine meals in the Fishermen's Club and restaurants at the docks, wolfed down freshly caught prawns straight off our barbecue and shortly before leaving enjoyed a wonderful meal on some friends' verandah with stunning views over the bay. Twofold Bay is a beautiful setting, surrounding the wharf with steep greenly covered hills that give onto a number of small beaches and inlets. The ambience is peaceful, the colours rich and strong. The permanent residents of Eden wharf are of course fishermen, who mostly put up with the inconvenience of visiting yachts with cheerful good humour and a willingness to give a hand. A hookah diver scraped our propeller and checked the hull before refusing any payment. Another neighbour spent some time on our outboard motor, a beast that was very close to being dumped at sea – only our respect for the ocean's

environment had saved it so far. The wharves also host a strolling parade of townsfolk and visitors, some fishing off the end, others just passing the time of day. It seemed all were in good humour, ready with a smile or a helpful word, interested to hear what others were doing and take pleasure in their enjoyment. Alastair, an adventurous young man on his tiny wooden yacht Warrane was heading north and we waved him off hoping to catch up later in our journey.

Overnight the wind returned to the south and 8am saw us on our way to our next port of call – Bermagui a small snug harbour famous for its marlin fishing. A yacht heading north along the NSW coast has to contend with the east coast current flowing south along the coast. At times it can reach four knots, although we have found one or two knots the norm. Today it seemed to have vanished and for a while we even picked up a north setting eddy. In any case we made better time than expected and had to wait off Bermagui for the making tide to give us enough water to enter the harbour. This we did shortly after 3pm, but not without a gentle nudge of the bottom on the way in. Again we were lucky with space at the jetty and we were directed to a comfortable birth by the harbour master. Adjacent was an exquisite wooden cruiser of some eighty feet built by the famous Norman Wright Shipyard in Brisbane and named Oceana – we complimented each other on the beauty of our boats and appropriateness of their names. As the sun slowly set behind a glowing horizon a number of fishermen cleaned their catch in the peaceful twilight before an audience of interested pelicans. Close by a fine restaurant was built out over the snug harbour and we dined on grilled baby snapper – fresh that morning.

Behind Snapper Island near Batemans Bay.

We left Bermagui on a three quarter tide, along with a number of small craft setting off for a days fishing. A light southerly was still with us and before long the morning haze had cleared, revealing the picturesque rocky coastline broken by numerous beaches, framed by green rolling hills and the dramatic hump of Mount Dromedary. We stayed close in, enjoying the beauty of the scene as we passed by at a steady seven knots. Again the current was not presenting too much of a problem. Before long we were off Broulee Island where we had anchored on our last trip southward, just short of our intended stopover at Batemans Bay. The names of the small villages we were passing, Mossy Point, Malua Bay, Potato Point, Sunpatch, all brought back many memories of holidaying in this part of the coast when Charlotte and Georgie were toddlers and we were living in Canberra. Mid afternoon we dropped the anchor behind Snapper Island, after assurances from a fisherman waiting to cross the bar into the Clyde River, that all would be well – the wind had veered to the east, but was still light. As twilight gave way to night the lights of Batemans Bay traced coloured patterns across the calm water while we enjoyed the ambience and the aroma of fish cooking in the barbecue. What would we do without it? Often a day's cruising ends with a yacht's safe arrival at an anchorage and the fact that the anchor is down is cause enough for celebrations. But there are other things that can enrich a day's end and make it a poignant and beautiful thing. It may be relief in refuge taken from a storm, an anchorage's special beauty, the colours of a sunset, the light on the water or some other magic dimension that enriches your soul and changes the ordinary to the sublime. Here, in an anchorage we had not lain in for many years, it was the echoes of old memories that still hovered in the dusk, the laughter of our children when they were young.

The fishing feet at Ulladulla dressed in their finest.

FISH ROLLS IN LEMON LEAVES

Joadja vineyard is located in Berrima a picturesque township in the southern highlands of NSW, an area known for its beautiful gardens and rich rolling farmlands. We enjoyed a number of their wines while ambling up the coast - particularly memorable was the Botrytis Autumn riesling made from selected late picked grapes and showing a lusciousness and a hint of delicate sweetness from some residual unfermented grape sugars and the naturally occurring botrytis. Also the 1999 Cabernet/Merlot a full bodied wine with rich cherry and plum characters.

Combine the following and then shape into firm, slightly flattened rolls. Sufficient flesh of chosen fish finely chopped, finely chopped garlic, finely chopped parsley, finely chopped spring onion, pinch of thyme, juice from 1 lemon, salt and pepper to taste, 1-2 eggs and enough plain flour to hold the rolls firm. Wrap each roll in a lemon leaf (secured by a toothpick) and cook over a low barbecue or bake in a moderate oven until cooked (approximately 10-12 minutes).

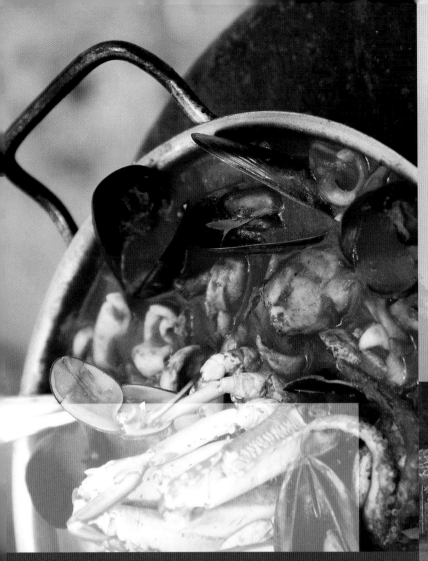

The rolling hills of the beautiful Shoalhaven Valley are home to Cambewarra Estate, a relatively new vineyard established by the Cole family in 1990. With the backdrop of the coastal ranges, often in winter mysteriously shrouded in mist or cloud the name Cambewarra, meaning 'misty mountain' evokes images of the old tribes that hunted and fished along the coastline for millennia. The maritime climate of the Shoalhaven, with cool moderate sea breezes during the ripening period allows the grape's entire characters to fully develop. Wines include Chardonnay, Cabinet Sauvignon, Chambourcin and Verdelho.

SPICEY SEAFOOD STEW

Heat ¾ cup of olive oil, 4 finely chopped cloves of garlic, 2 chopped onions, 2 chopped chillies, 4 peeled tomatoes, diced octopus pieces, available fish heads. Simmer for 15 minutes, remove fish heads and discard. Add 1-2 cups of white wine, ¼ cup red wine vinegar, sufficient small potatoes in their jackets, and simmer for a further 10 minutes, add fish chunks, peas or beans and simmer for a further 6-7 minutes. Add cooked mussels, crayfish chunks, salt and pepper to taste and simmer for a minute or so until they are reheated. Serve in deep bowls with crusty bread and a full bodied wine.

BLESSING OF THE FLEET

Ulladulla

The 'hole in the wall', tucked away against the southern shore of Jervis Bay, is a favourite stopover for yachts.

BATEMANS BAY TO ULLADULLA

By morning the wind had risen enough to build up a swell that was breaking with some force on the Tollgate Islands and the reefs on the northern headland, where rock fisherman appeared to be fishing from suicidal positions. Perhaps the angle we looked from distorted the picture. Despite the lumpy sea recreational fishermen were out in force in a wide variety of craft, fishing the deeper offshore reefs and the edge of the warm southern current. There must have been twenty or more craft off Brush Island alone and there was plenty of activity apparent. A passing squall of rain and a rising wind did nothing to dampen the enthusiasm. We were heading for Ulladulla, a man-made harbour in an indentation in the coast behind Warden Head. For many years it was an important port of call when coastal steamers still serviced the coast. It is still home to a large fishing fleet. By the time we had picked up the harbour leads there was quite a heavy sea running, producing large breaks on Sullivans Reef and on the bombora on the northern headland. A strong wind warning had been issued and we were glad to enter the calm of the harbour, protected by its great stone breakwaters. We tied alongside a large steel trawler.

kiama headland

The square rigger "Our Sven" on the slip at Wollongong

ULLADULLA TO PORT HACKING

We left Ulladulla in the early afternoon after a layover to enjoy the 'Blessing of the Fleet'. Also, as the harbour held some old family memories we wanted to wander around a little. We have an old sepia photograph, taken 80 odd years ago, of Rob's parents boating on the harbour and much later in the 1960's we used to visit Mollymook, a nearby beach. This time the town and harbour were crowded but happy places to be, with the fishing fleet decked out with bunting and a large colourful parade with the local Italian community to the fore. The unfortunate outboard motor, having escaped the depths of the ocean was donated to the local Volunteer Coastal Patrol who eventually managed to bring it to life. Later we received a letter to tell us they had successfully auctioned it, bringing in some funds for an organisation that provides an essential safety net. Along with the Volunteer Coast Guard and Volunteer Marine Rescue these volunteers give up much of their time to make the waters of Australia's coast a safer place. And we thank them for it.

A quiet corner of Wollongong Harbour

The south-easterly had moderated somewhat but had left a large uncomfortable swell running and there was plenty of broken water as we were going out. It was only a three-hour run to Jervis Bay and as we approached the entrance we were reminded of the last time we had sailed north. It had been just after dawn and our son-in-law, Simon Merchant, who had been trolling a line all the way from Hobart with very limited success, gave a hoot of delight as his line started to run out under a heavy strain. Obviously a monster. Shortly after, much to Simon's disgust the line broke. Moments later the offending submarine surfaced. Much laughter. Towards dusk we anchored off the "Hole in the Wall", one of our favourite anchorages on the south coast. The foreshore here is heavily timbered right down to the edge of beaches that line the inside of the bay. The protected water was hardly ruffled and divers and fishermen were out in force while children played in the shallows. The sea was still very lumpy in the morning, particularly as we cleared Point Perpendicular, which in the grey morning light was nearly as forbidding as the coast around Tasman Island. We went well out

LINGUINE WITH MARINARA SAUCE

Heat 2 finely chopped cloves of garlic and 2 sliced chillies in ½ cup of olive oil for 3-4 minutes over a medium heat. Add one cup of chicken stock and increase the heat to high so that the oil and the stock emulsify. Reduce by half. Add a dozen or so mussels (washed and cleaned) and cook until the shells open. Add 200gm of diced whiting (or similar) fillets and cook for 1 minute. Add 200gm of peeled and de-veined prawns and cook for 1 minute. Add 200gm of scallops and cook for 2 minutes. Season to taste.

Pour the sauce onto 500gm cooked linguine, add freshly chopped parsley and toss before serving.

The Sydney skyline lifts out of the tossing sea.

to avoid the Sir John Young shoals and despite the southerly current continued to make good time, the log hovering around seven knots. The day gradually improved to near perfect. Clear blue skies highlighted the beautiful coast near Gerringong and Kiama and a moderate south-westerly gradually flattened the sea. Oceania loved it. We had intended to overnight at Wollongong but as northerlies were predicted the next day, and we were going so well, we decided to push on to Port Hacking, which we reached shortly after 4 pm. Rather than anchor near the entrance at Jibbon Beach we decided to risk the shallow entrance into Gunnamatta Bay, which was more protected. An unwise decision as it turned out. The channel had silted by about half a meter from the depths marked on our chart and we were temporarily embarrassed until a very kind police boat helped pull us free. We anchored off Jibbon beach after all, with only our pride any the worse for wear.

Sydney CBD from Watsons Bay

A lighthouse at the entrance to Sydney Harbour

PORT HACKING TO SYDNEY

Another perfect day with a light north-easter ruffling the sparkling water and the sun highlighting the colours of the coast – the red tiled roofs, green parks and golf courses, granite cliffs and the shimmering whiteness of the famous southern beaches – Maroubra, Coogee, Bronte and Bondi. Arriving at Sydney Harbour is always an event to remember.

The Sydney skyline behind the sun worshippers at Lady Beach.

 The sail along the rocky cliffs lined with houses, the occasional glimpses of the towering CBD skyline, and finally the entrance through the heads into a mighty harbour with one of the world's most exciting cities holding it in a close embrace. We had both spent part of our youth here and although it is many years since we have lived permanently it still always feels like coming home. Sydney is one of the great sailing destinations and has a presence as powerful as Port Davey or the Hinchinbrook Channel and can be as much fun to sail as the Whitsundays.

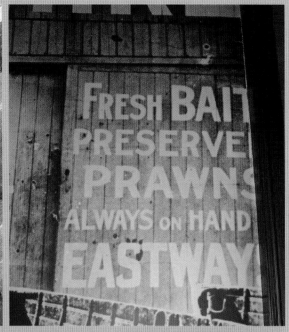

Boil squid (50gm) cleaned and cut into rings for approximately one hour. In a deep serving dish heat ¼ cup of Spanish olive oil, add 1 tomato, peeled, seeded and chopped, 2 tablespoons tomato paste, ½ brown onion, chopped, 1 clove garlic, finely chopped, 2-3 bay leaves, stir well and add 50gm green prawns, shelled, 500gm green mud crab cut into 3 pieces, squid, 3-4 mussels, 200gm of white fish cut in pieces. Stir all again, then add ¼ cup water, ¾ cup of dry white wine, ½ teaspoon paprika, salt and pepper and stir. Cook slowly for ten minutes after the ingredients have come to the boil. Serve in the pot you cooked it in with a dish of hot fluffy rice sprinkled with saffron or lightly dusted with paprika and finely chopped parsley.

DOYLES

PAELLA

As a boarder at nearby Rose Bay Convent Rosemary remembers spending many a Sunday, with her sister Viv, at Camp Cove with the Duncan family. One of the great treats was to be taken to Doyles for fish and chips. Well over forty years later this treat is just as memorable. With Oceania anchored in the bay we often sat amongst the seagulls on the beach or around the white clothed tables, relishing what this renowned establishment is so famous for whilst enjoying the spectacular views. We also shared Doyles wonderful seafood platter pictured.

Brewed by the Malt Shovel Brewery in Camperdown NSW this beer is named after the legendary James Squire - a highwayman who was deported to the infant penal colony at NSW and became its first brewer of note, producing a range of beers at Kissing Point in 1795. The India Pale Ale is made with only Munich and pale malt and is brewed to a rich golden colour, with a robust malty character. Its earthy floral aromas are a result of dry-hopping with English Fuggles hops added to the maturation tanks. The original India Ales were brewed in London in the 1790's, with added hops and high alcohol contact to survive the long trip in square riggers, through the tropics of both the Atlantic and Pacific Oceans, to India.

PRAWNS IN WHITE WINE

In a large pot simmer the following. 1 bottle of dry white wine, 4 sliced spring onions, 2 sliced carrots and an equal portion of chopped leek, 4 cloves of crushed garlic, 2 sliced chillies, dash of paprika. Add thyme, parsley, and salt and pepper to taste. After 15 minutes add 250gm prawns per plate and boil for a further 2/3 minutes by which time the prawns should be a tempting red. Serve in bowls with crusty bread.

Some of Australia's most expensive real estate.

Rose Bay-Kincoppel

We were planning to spend a month or so here interspersed with trips home. Dave and Jill Henry had arranged a mooring for us in Snails Bay, in front of their home on Long Nose Point. After dropping anchor for a leisurely lunch below Rosemary's old school at Rose Bay we cruised on through the harbour and picked up the mooring in the late afternoon and with a pang realised this leg of the trip was over.

SARDINES WITH GARLIC AND BREAD CRUMBS

Rinse and dry a sufficient quantity of sardines. Toss in salt and pepper and arrange in a baking dish brushed with olive oil. Sprinkle sardines with chopped garlic, parsley, and lemon juice to taste. Add 1/3 cup of dry white wine and top with bread crumbs. Bake at 185c for around 18-20 minutes.

Over the next few days Bluey left for Canberra and Don and Sue for Hobart. After spending a short while with the Henry's and enjoying nearby Balmain we followed them, planning to return in time to farewell Dave and Jill on their circumnavigation cruise in their beautiful yacht Sweet Chariot. May saw us back in Sydney and a couple of days later we waved the Henry's off and prepared to enjoy what the harbour had to offer. The late autumn weather was wonderful and on most evenings we could enjoy the last of the sun sitting on the aft deck as we waited for night to settle and for the city lights to bathe the harbour in their dazzling display. In due course we moved to an anchorage at Double Bay, and then to Watsons Bay where we enjoyed great seafood at Doyles restaurant, one of Sydney's icon eateries, and leisurely walks around the beautiful foreshores. Every day brought a passing parade of the sea and for a change it was only a short dinghy ride to the city or the eastern suburbs.

Sydney Harbour Bridge

FISHBURN

Sydney Ferries

(Opposite) fish markets. (Above) An old work boat heads out for another day of toil on the harbour.

MV Reliance in Snails Bay.

The Bathers Pavilion Restaurant occupies a beautiful old art deco building that was indeed, in days gone by, a bathers pavilion. It is in a great setting, overlooking the golden sands of Balmoral Beach and the turquoise waters of the harbour to 'the heads'. After dining, there are fine walks along the foreshore and plenty of spots to relax and enjoy the ambience of this very special place.

This is one of a number of fine dishes we have enjoyed there.

Blanch a 2ml thick slice of parsnip in olive oil and lay along a jewfish fillet and set aside.

Prepare a spinach spaetzle by blending baby spinach leaves, separating the fluid with slight warming and retaining the solid chlorophyll. Blend the chlorophyll and 6 whole eggs with 375gm flour, add 180ml cream and beat well for 2 3 minutes. Add some milk if the mixture is too stiff. Leave spaetzle to rest for 30 minutes before cooking. To cook push the spaetzle through a steamer tray to create little droplets into salted boiling water. When cooked refresh with iced water.

Pan fry the jewfish, with the parsnip side down first in a little olive oil and then bake in a hot oven for 6-8 minutes.

In the meantime heat up horseradish cream, and pan fry the spaetzle folding through some baby spinach leaves.

Place the spaetzle in the centre of four plates and spoon over the horseradish cream.

Place the cooked fish on top and drizzle with beetroot jus.
Serves 4

BATHERS PAVILION

JEWFISH WITH PARSNIP CRUST

Yachts on Pittwater

northern nsw

Pittwater near Scotland Island.

North Head, leaving Sydney Harbour

Long Reef Beach, Sydney's northern beaches.

SYDNEY TO BROKEN BAY

Our last night in Sydney Harbour was spent anchored in Spring Cove, a lovely spot just around from the old Quarantine Station on North Head. Most of the foreshore is lush green reserve framing the whiteness of the Store Beach, still washed by water from the spring in the hillside above that gave the cove its name in 1788. Across the bay the rocky foreshore of Dobroyd Head was deserted and there was no sign of life in the Sydney Harbour National Park. It is a remarkably peaceful anchorage for one surrounded by a big city. A front crossed in the night leaving brisk south westerlies for our run up to Broken Bay and we were underway with a reefed main and genoa at 8.30 am. As usual we stayed close in to enjoy the views of the coastline and the many places that held memories for both of us. Rob's family had lived along the northern beaches when he was a teenager and there were few beaches we passed that did not bring back memories of summers long passed. Rosemary, while still a newly arrived Irish colleen, had often holidayed with friends at Whale Beach. After rounding Barrenjoey Head we crossed Broken Bay and anchored in Refuge Bay for a late lunch. This we enjoyed while basking in warm sunshine, protected from the wind by the enveloping sandstone hills. Over the next few days we idled round to Pittwater, spending some nights in Lovett Bay before picking up a mooring at the Royal Prince Alfred Yacht Club and preparing again to return to Hobart. Georgina was not far off birthing her first son, Joseph, an event we were all greatly looking forward to.

PITTWATER TO PORT STEPHENS

Two months later we arrived back at the 'Alfred' content in the knowledge that Joseph had come safely into the world to join his cousins Hubert and Rufus. Oceania had been brought alongside D finger, a pleasant surprise that made preparations for the next leg much easier. We had enjoyed our stay at this most hospitable of clubs, they had gone out of their way to make us feel at home, as we are sure they do all visiting yachts. The next day Don and Sue Clark arrived to join us again and by nightfall all was in order for a departure and we were able to retire to the clubhouse for 'happy hour' followed by dinner overlooking the marina and Pittwater. Late on Saturday afternoon we cast off with Lance Grant (Sue's brother-in-law) joining us on board and we motored through the western passage beside Scotland Island, past Lovett Bay and Towlers Bay to the calm waters of beautiful Coasters Retreat, protected from a fresh southerly by the heavily wooded Soldiers Point. Although it was several degrees warmer than Tasmania there was still a touch of winter in the air and by 6 pm darkness had settled on the water and soon after the cook was left to himself with the barbecue on the aft deck. We were up at 4 am ready for an early departure for Port Stephens, a leg of nearly eighty nautical miles. First light was still two hours away and it was a black and chilly morning. Fumbling around in the darkness we had hoisted the mainsail before flashes of lightning out to sea behind the Palm Beach peninsula persuaded us that some caution was called for and the first reef was put in before motoring off the anchor-

BAKED EGGPLANT
STUFFED WITH PRAWNS

In the semi-tropical environment around the shores of Port Stephens you can watch eggplants grow, and prawns spawning in the rivers that run into the bay have always been abundant.

Remove the flesh from sufficient eggplants, leaving 5/6mm of flesh and being careful not to break the shell. Brush the interior of the eggplant shells with olive oil and bake in a preheated barbecue oven (use a baking dish if over direct coals or gas). Prepare the stuffing by simmering the following for 10 minutes in white wine; the eggplant flesh, finely chopped garlic and peppers, a pinch of thyme, a few black olives, salt and pepper, all to taste. Drain and combine prawns (or Tasmanian scallops, or cubes of any reasonably firm fish) with the stuffing. Spoon into the shells, sprinkle with Parmesan cheese and bake for a further 5/6 minutes until the cheese is golden brown.

We sampled a number of Hunter Valley wines, some well known, others not so, as we progressed up the NSW coast. It is one of the world's great wine making regions, and just as much as the famous German valleys of the Rhine and the Mosselle it produces wines with its own special characteristics. The two classic white varieties of the valley are chardonnay and semillon and we were impressed by the Tyrrells Old Winery 2002 Chardonnay Semillon. This wine has a soft, full bodied chardonnay fruit mid palate and a crisp citrus semillon finish. Despite its youth and the hard cellaring conditions in the bilge it was an excellent accompaniment to the full range of dishes aboard - from simple barbecue to spicy asian.

The waterfall at Refuge Bay

Pittwater

A quiet canal frontage in Pittwater

age. Daylight found us well out to sea below a dull grey sky with small patches of storm cloud to the east and inland behind the coast near Ettalong. During the morning the sky cleared somewhat and with a fresh southerly building we were soon surging along under main, mizzen and genoa and keeping an eye on the occasional squalls that blew up from behind. By early afternoon the grey prominences of Yacaaba and Tomare Heads, marking the entrance to Port Stephens, began to peep over the horizon. By dusk we had edged into Shoal Bay, the first anchorage inside the port, and dropped anchor in four meters over a clean sandy bottom. The entrance into Port Stephens is spectacular. The high rocky headlands, the nearby

On Scotland Island

islands of Boondelbah and Cabbage Tree and the ruggedly beautiful foreshore between Point Stephens and Tomaree Head washed by heavy breaks from the southerly swell. It was good to be back in the waters of this extensive harbour that we had first visited in a sailer trailer thirty years before. Then we had spent a month here and in the Myall Lakes, which are joined to it by the Myall River at Tea Gardens. The years seemed to disappear as we sailed these beautiful waters once again and the memories came flooding back; bathing in the fresh warm water of the lakes, the Christmas tree we decorated on the shore with flour and foil paper, Georgie receiving a battery operated 'Baby That A Way' from Santa, an unsuitable present on a boat…now she has her own live 'Baby That A Way'…. and Charlotte has two.

Beaches, headlands and bays around Port Stephens

Port Stephens

The weather had improved overnight and we were greeted by warm sunshine and sparkling water that was so clear we felt we could reach over and scoop a handful of the fine white sand lying over the anchor chain. We motored around the southern shore, passing a number of small beaches nestled between rocky headlands and the township of Nelsons Bay crowding around a bustling marina, to the 'Anchorage Marina' at Corlette Point where we planned to overnight. In the evening we had dinner with Don's cousin Peter Foster (by the longest coincident a fellow groomsman at Rob's brother's wedding forty years before) and his wife Jane. On Tuesday Peter kindly took us on a guided tour and later we sailed to Fame Cove, a delightful anchorage on the northern shore surrounded by heavily forested hills. The planned two nights stay drew into three as we waited for strong northerlies to abate and watched a pair of sea eagles busily refurbishing their nest, overlooking us from a high eucalypt on the shore. Mostly we shared the quiet of the anchorage with only one or two other boats and in the mornings and early evenings nothing disturbed our enjoyment of the symphony of birdcalls. White galahs relaxed without concern adjacent to the sea eagles nest as the great birds came and went.

PORT STEPHENS TO CROWDY HEAD

The wind finally returned to the south and despite a strong wind warning we decided to make the short hop to Sugarloaf Bay, an enchanting anchorage off the small fishing village of Seal Rocks, twenty five miles to the north. With reefed main and jib we reached past the eastern shore of Broughton Island, part of the Myall Lakes national park and eight miles off Port Stephens, with the wind blowing a steady twenty-five knots. There are a number of remote and sheltered anchorages on the island where a yacht can over-night and avoid the need of putting in to Port Stephens. Here you can enjoy the solitude of an uninhabited off shore island and walk untrodden sandy beaches with the tang of seaweed strong in the breeze and gulls wheeling overhead. Further on, midway between the island and Sugarloaf Point the high rocks from which the township of Seal Rocks takes its name became visible against the tumbling mass of grey water, but it was not until we were much closer that we sighted the dangerous protrusion

Early morning beside the jetty at Crowdy Head

of Little Seal Rock, a trap for the unwary lying two miles off the point. Rosemary, who is a great chef in normal circumstances, is unsurpassed in rough weather. With the galley angled at forty-five degrees, surging up and down over five meters as the southerly swells rolled up behind us she miraculously produced freshly toasted fingers of cheese, tomato and salmon crisped with hot mustard, and pots of freshly brewed coffee for lunch. With our appetites sharpened by the chill wind and the exhilaration of the sail nothing could have tasted better. The wind was now gusting over thirty knots and the protection of Sugarloaf Bay was very welcome after rounding the point and edging close up to the beach under Statis Rocks. A swell invaded the anchorage but Oceania rode comfortably with the whistling wind holding her stern into the swell. For most of the night the wind tore at the rigging and even with our 120 lb plough anchor well pulled in and fifty meters of chain out we spent a restless night with frequent radar checks. By the morning the wind had veered to the west somewhat and the long ledge of Statis Rock was now an unwelcome lee shore.

Smokey Cape Lighthouse

By morning the wind had eased a little and from time to time the sun broke through the chasing clouds, turning the waters of the bay into translucent greens and blues. It was calm enough inside the bay for a fisherman in a small dinghy to troll along the face of Statis Rocks. Outside a large sea was still running, the white caps at times gleaming and inviting, but grey and bleak when the dark clouds covered the sun. In mid morning we recovered the anchor and laid a course for Crowdy Heads to see us at the entrance to the harbour, which has only two meters at low water, with the rising tide close to full. In the last hour of daylight after giving Forde Rock a wide clearance we tied up to the jetty, once again glad to be out of the swell. But our relief was short lived as the surge alongside was most uncomfortable and at times we feared for the safety of the hull as we were buffeted against the piles. It was a different Crowdy Head this time to when we were last there twelve years ago. Then we had bought seafood from the local co-op and sat on deck in the burning sun drinking champagne and peeling prawns. This time we fell into our beds exhausted as the wind howled around us and the halyards rattled.

BAKED BLUE SWIMMER CRABS

One of Rob's favourite pastimes as a boy growing up on the central coast of New South Wales was fishing for Blue Swimmer Crabs. Using any piece of meat as bait the crabs were lured to within reach of the surface and scooped up with a landing net. Watching the crabs as they were pulled to the surface through the clear blue water, waiting apprehensively for them to drop off before they were within reach, never lost its thrill. They are delicious eating simply boiled and chilled, but this is a dish that is unsurpassed and avoids the diner needing to fight with claws and shells.

Remove crab meat from 4 reasonably sized crabs and retain the top shell. In a pan melt sufficient butter; add the juice off one lemon, a teaspoon of English mustard, a pinch of nutmeg and a pinch of paprika. Remove from the heat and gently stir in the crab meat. Spoon the mixture into the shells. Mix sufficient bread crumbs with melted butter and add grated cheddar cheese and spoon the topping over the crab meat. Bake at 200c until golden brown (approximately 10/12 minutes).

John Cruikshank established Callatoota Estate in the Hunter Valley at Wybong in 1973, after the noted Spanish historian Don Salvador de Madariaga convinced John that for his good health he should drink more wine. Around 120 tonnes of grapes are harvested with styles ranging from elegant rosé to full bodied reds matured in underground cellars in American and French oak casks. We enjoyed the chilled rosé, with its crisp finish and excellent Cabernet character with a number of seafood dishes during our time in Port Stephens and when our inclination was to sample some heavier reds we savoured some bottles of Callatoota's magnificent Cabernet Sauvignons while being sure to keep some others to sample further up the coast. John produces several styles of Cab Sav ranging from the lighter 'free run' to the more full bodied. We found his 'pressings' as being aptly described as a wine 'fit for heroes.'

Among the wines enjoyed at anchorages north of the Hunter Valley were some Rothvale Vineyard's whites, including the 2000 unwooded Chardonnay and the 2000 Semillon Chardonnay. Both are made from hand picked grapes from well established vines, in the case of the chardonnay 34 years, and the varietal integrity of the wines comes through in the aromas and tastes. The chardonnay, made with a long slow fermentation has a tropical fruit bouquet and citrus aromas and a fine long lasting palate with the honey, fruit and the acid balance giving a well rounded finish. The semillon Chardonnay was also excellent with a lively refreshing finish that left the palate with subtle tropical fruit flavours. The winerey lies beneath the Brokenback Range near Pokolbin, one of Australia's premium wine growing areas, and one that should not be left off the itinery. Another favourite was the 1999 Absent Friends Unoaked Chardonnay from the Peacock Hill Vineyard.

PRAWNS IN GARLIC BREAD CRUMBS

Clean King Prawns, brush with olive oil, toss in seasoned bread crumbs (mix bread crumbs finely chopped garlic and parsley, chilli flakes, salt and pepper all in amounts to taste), ensure all the prawns are well coated. Place in an oiled dish and bake in an oven preheated to 190c until they are a tempting red (about 10 minutes).

Looking south from Smokey Cape

CROWDY HEAD TO COFFS HARBOUR

The wind, which had been forecast to ease, remained stubbornly high but in the morning we were glad to be off the jetty as soon as there was enough water over the entrance. The shoals to the north of the harbour in Crowdy Bay were covered with breaking water as we made a good offing before resuming our course north east to Trial Bay. Away to the west the familiar face of Point Perpendicular guarded the entrance to the beautiful Camden Haven River and a few hours sail saw us off Port Macquarie with the wind still over our stern. The southerly continued unabated through the day, rolling large swells under our stern and chasing the scudding clouds across the sun. By late in the afternoon it became apparent that we would not reach Trial Bay by nightfall and opted instead for refuge behind Korogoro Point at Hat Head. Although a number of times in the past we had planned to anchor at Hat Head circumstances had prevented us from doing so. So as we nosed around the point and into the bay it was with the anticipation always felt when entering a new anchorage. Would it be one of those enchanted places whose memory remains forever locked in your heart? Finally we anchored over a sandy bottom and spent the last of the twilight enjoying the beauty of the high rocky headland and the sweep of the long white beach.

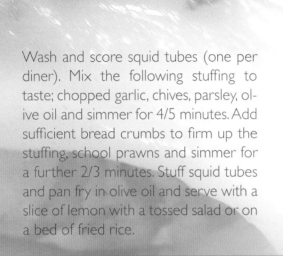

Wash and score squid tubes (one per diner). Mix the following stuffing to taste; chopped garlic, chives, parsley, olive oil and simmer for 4/5 minutes. Add sufficient bread crumbs to firm up the stuffing, school prawns and simmer for a further 2/3 minutes. Stuff squid tubes and pan fry in olive oil and serve with a slice of lemon with a tossed salad or on a bed of fried rice.

SQUID WITH PRAWN, GARLIC AND PARSLEY STUFFING

While anchored in Trial Bay we rescued a few more fine Hunter Valley wines from our cellar in the bilge, including a memorable 1999 Gewurztraminer from the Caper-caillie Wine Company situated near Lovedale. Made in a modern winery from well established vines the wine exemplified the spicy and aromatic qualities of the variety and a thorough search was made of the dark and cavernous bilge to ensure that none were overlooked.

SNAPPER WITH CHILLI AND GINGER

There are many ways to cook snapper as pictured above but a simple way is:

Stuff a good-sized snapper with layers of thinly sliced limes and ginger. Place the snapper on oiled foil and cook in a hot oven for about 20 minutes. While cooking baste the skin of the fish with a garnish made of a tablespoon of peanut oil, some grated ginger, crushed garlic, palm sugar sliced chilli and lime juice to taste.

Our night was disturbed by the southerly swell wrapping around the point and invading our anchorage. With strong winds forecast to continue we decided to motor around Smokey Cape to the more protected waters of Trial Bay. Once outside we were greeted by a very lumpy and uncomfortable swell and a grim and foreboding sky. Smokey Cape, shrouded in cloud and rain, was an awe-inspiring sight as it came and went behind dark rolling clouds and the veils of passing showers. By the time we had given the off lying rocks a wide berth those on deck were soaked and wondering again where the warm weather had gone. Rounding Laggers Point, dominated by the imposing stone ruins of the old Trial Bay Gaol, we were greeted by the wide, smooth expanse of the bay. Soon the skies cleared and although the wind was still blowing a gale we were once again happy with our lot and were soon absorbed in a large breakfast of pancakes and fruit. Later we took the opportunity to visit the town of South West Rocks, enjoying a lovely position looking north over the sweep of the beach, and the lighthouse on Smokey Cape. Situated on a point below Big Smokey the lighthouse provides one of the most dramatic and beautiful views along the coast. Rugged hills running to a rocky foreshore broken by small sand fringed bays. To the south mile after mile of beach and tossing ocean.

Up and away early for Coffs Harbour. The dawn cloud soon gave way to a sparkling morning as we ran before a moderate southwesterly. After some hours of beautiful sailing patches of storm cloud began to form in the distance and an hour out of Coffs we were overtaken by squalls and rain. Once again we were soaked and the sea sullen and white capped and we were glad to surf into the relatively quiet waters behind the breakwater. Winds were still gusting over thirty and by nightfall we had registered forty-seven knots from the east. Berthing was difficult with the wind gusting across our berth and threatening to blow us onto a beautiful motor cruiser sharing our marina bay. Coming in too fast we gave the marina a good solid thump before the reverse thrust pulled us up. Many black looks from the crew who were shamed by the incompetence of the helmsman. But none the less we were all glad to be in Coffs and not at one of the open roadstead anchorages along the coast. Coffs is a favourite stopover, the only virtual all weather port between the Gold Coast Seaway and Port Stephens, and sitting on a part of the coast where fertile and picturesque mountains run right to the sea. Our plan was to spend some time here to catch up with Colin and Jill Rosewarne (Ro's sister and husband) and other friends. Within a day the winds had swung around to the north, bringing with them the warm and balmy weather one expects on the north coast.

small beaches nestled below Smokey Cape

COFFS HARBOUR TO SOUTHPORT.

Although strong northerlies kept us in Coffs longer than we intended we thoroughly enjoyed every moment of our stay. The beautiful walks to Mutton Bird Island where the first of the migratory birds were arriving back from the northern hemisphere to mate and breed; along Coffs Creek where a boardwalk meanders amongst the mangroves and tidal flats; and along miles and miles of gleaming beaches washed by the pounding surf. There are a number of restaurants within a short stroll of the harbour and we enjoyed fine food al fresco as darkness settled and the passing parade eddied around us. Lance and Jan Grant and Margaret Jackson over-nighted, after an electrical storm forced them to land their plane in transit to Sydney. The docks bustled with the activities of the fishing fleet, unloading the catch in the early mornings and returning to their toil each evening.

Fishermans Wharf, Coffs Harbour

During our stopover in Coffs we had the opportunity of enjoying some of the reds we had collected on the way, but due to the exigencies of sailing, had not had the chance of sampling. We found the Callatoota Estate Cabernet Franc luscious, with opulent fruit flavours and a full textual palate and very much enjoyed the blended 'Two Cabernets', a rich and complex wine with strong mouth filling fruit flavours. Perhaps the favourite on the aft deck, when the gentle evening northerly mixed the aromas of the rich hinterland and the tang of the nearby Coral Sea, was the 2001 Shiraz, with its taste of spicy berry fruits enhanced by subtle oaking. Or then again, perhaps it was the elegantly structured 1999 Show Reserve Cabernet Sauvignon with its supple tannin finish.

FISH SALAD WITH AN ASIAN TWIST

Blanch 200gm of sugar snap peas, drain and rinse under cold water and combine with 3 Lebanese cucumbers seeded and sliced, 1 red capsicum seeded and sliced thinly, 4 spring onions thinly sliced, 1 cup bean sprouts, sugar snap peas and mint in a large bowl and mix.

Dressing: Combine 2 tablespoons of lemon juice; 1 tablespoon of olive oil, 1 tablespoon sesame oil, 1 tablespoon soy sauce, 2 tablespoons chopped fresh coriander in a jar and shake.

Cook boneless fish pieces on a heated oiled pan or barbecue plate. Drizzle dressing over salad and toss gently. On each plate arrange salad and top with fish. Drizzle remaining dressing over fish. Garnish with fresh herbs.

Pictured: Mitsuo from Kabuki by the Sea

Moderating northerlies, forecast to back to the south during the day, gave us an opportunity to head north again and we departed mid morning, planning to arrive off Byron Bay at dawn the following day. The light north-easterlies had flattened the sea and with tightly sheeted sails we were able to lay South Solitary Island, giving the dangerous reefs closer in a wide birth. The sun was out, sparkling on the water and a welcome change from the weather that had brought us up to Coffs. Further out a whale was 'blowing', around us dolphins chased beneath our bows, shearwaters skimmed amongst the waves, and the occasional gull investigated our wake before circling off. By mid afternoon we were clear of North Solitary Island and as the wind backed we steered for Evans Head, planning to sail closer in on a port tack once the wind came around to the northwest. Nightfall brought the wind from the west and shortly afterwards the lights of the fishing fleets began to glow in the darkness, strung across our front like a chain of fireflies. As the night passed the wind continued to back and we were able to ease our sheets as we wound our way through the fishing fleets of Evans Head and Ballina. Overhead the heavens were ablaze and as we neared Cape Byron the first gentle fragrances of the tropics drifted to us across the water. Going north it can be hard work to clear Cape Byron, as the East Coast Current always seems to be running south at a great

Coffs Creek

rate. On our first trip north we spent almost all of one night trying to 'inch' past, making only one or two knots across the ground. Tonight it was a different story, making six to seven knots in beautiful conditions, and we had cleared the Cape before the first sun's rays struck the tall tower of the lighthouse. There is a picturesque anchorage off the beach under Cape Byron, the eastern tip of Australia, that gives somewhat tenuous shelter from southerlies. Ashore the township provides beautiful and relaxed surroundings and a wide choice of excellent restaurants, more than usual with a strong Asian influence. The views from the lighthouse, a beacon we normally seemed to pass in the night, are superb and in the clear waters below we watched the steady passage of whales and the sinister shadow of a shark as it hunted around the reefs. Pressing on while the steady wind stayed in the south we continued our run north. The steep ridges of the border ranges and the distinctive profile of Mount Warning, named by Cook to warn of the dangerous reefs ahead, lined the western horizon and were silhouetted against a perfect sky. Ahead the high rises of first Coolangatta

A distant Smokey Cape

A prawn trawler off Evans Head

and then the Gold Coast came into view. We stayed well off as we approached Point Danger to make sure we avoided the reefs, before altering our course to the Gold Coast Seaway. By nightfall we were happily berthed at the Marina Mirage – a long time favourite of ours that is blessed with many fine restaurants and is only a short stroll across the spit to Main Beach. Arrivals and departures are a special part of each cruise. It's great to cast off the lines and head into the blue, full of anticipation of what's to come. But it's hard to beat the satisfaction of arriving safely and having Oceania 'snugged down' in a destination you know you will enjoy. It was wonderful to be met at the Marina by Michael and Diana Battle, our best man and bridesmaid at our wedding in New Guinea in 1966. The years since vanished as we sat on the aft deck reminiscing and later enjoying a fine meal at their apartment close by. Ro's brother Eugene joined us the following night and again far too many celebratory wines were drunk. Eugene had sailed with us twelve years before on a trip from Southport to Mooloolaba. Later both Charlotte and Georgie and their families flew up to join us. Teaching Hubie how to surf and watching Rufus and Joseph enjoy life on board have been some of life's great gifts.

Cliffs at Cape Byron

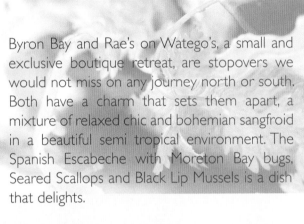

Byron Bay and Rae's on Watego's, a small and exclusive boutique retreat, are stopovers we would not miss on any journey north or south. Both have a charm that sets them apart, a mixture of relaxed chic and bohemian sangfroid in a beautiful semi tropical environment. The Spanish Escabeche with Moreton Bay bugs, Seared Scallops and Black Lip Mussels is a dish that delights.

Finely slice 1 Spanish onion, 1 clove of garlic, 2 baby fennel, 1 large carrot, 1 medium leek, 1 red capsicum.

In a large saucepan, on medium to high heat, add a good splash of olive oil. Sauté all vegetables hot and fast, constantly stirring for one minute. Next pour in about 1 cup of good quality white wine vinegar and toss in 150gm white sugar. When boiling add ½ teaspoon of saffron. Stir for 30 seconds and then take it off the heat. Stir ½ cup of olive oil to cool the mixture and to lock in the crisp colourful flavours of the vegetables.

Take the shell off one large Moreton Bay Bug, leaving only the meat. Sear the bug tail for 1½ minutes in a heavy frying pan, add 3 scallops, 3 black lip mussels, cover the pan and cook for 1 more minute. Stand for 30 seconds.

Add seafood to escabeche, fold in some fresh basil leaves, chervil, tarragon, flat leaf parsely. Serve immediately.

RAE'S ON WATEGO'S

SPANISH ESCABECHE WITH MORETON BAY BUGS

Byron Bay

Main Beach, Southport.

south east queensland

Lifesavers, Main Beach

SOUTHPORT TO MOOLOOLABA

The next passage north offers an attractive alternative to the quite lengthy ocean passage to Mooloolaba. Behind the protective bulk of the Stradbroke Islands a number of narrow channels wind through dozens of smaller islands packed close together at the southern end of Moreton Bay. Once the broad expanse of the bay is reached a route may be chosen along its western shore with stops at a number of snug marinas, or depending on the weather, along the eastern side of the bay beside the sandy shores of North Stradbroke and Moreton Islands. However this inland route is not without its difficulties as the waters are shallow and strewn with sand banks. Being averse to grounding we thought it prudent to enlist the services of Brian Ross, a charter skipper we had become friendly with, and cast off from the marina to take the high tide through the shallowest patch below Jacobs Well. It was just on first light, but before long the sun rose in a cloudless sky and the dull grey of morning gave way to a shining blue sky and sparkling waters. We had calculated that we would have ten centimeters to spare, but in fact going over half an hour before full tide we had to slide the keel over the mud for thirty meters before we made the deeper water. As there was not a higher tide for another two weeks we were more than a little relieved to have made it and not sentenced to perhaps a lengthy grounding. As we slowly motored along the winding channels we passed small

Palazzo Versace

For some time we lived on board Oceania as she was berthed at the Marina Mirage in front of the Palazzo Versace. Whilst there we enjoyed a number of meals at this grand establishment. Vanitas restaurant is world renowned with an absolutely mouth watering menu and a glorious setting.

Make a guacamole by blending 2 avocados with 50gm of sour cream, 1 lime (juiced and grated). When smooth fold through 2 golden shallots finely grated, 2 peeled and diced tomatoes, 1 red chilli finely diced, season and fold through plenty of crab meat so that it is just bound by the guacamole.

Press crab mixture into a tall ring mould and push out onto the centre of a large bowl. Top with candied red capsicum and a quenelle of avruga roe and a piece of chervil. Foam up some yellow gazpacho and pour around the tian.

To make 6 serves of gazpacho foam macerate 15 blanched and quartered Roma tomatoes, 2 diced yellow capsicums, 1 chopped cucumber, 1 chopped small red onion, 1 sliced clove of garlic, 50ml champagne vinegar, 1 slice sourdough bread (cubed), dash of tabasco sauce, 30ml extra virgin olive oil, sea salt. Let sit for 6 hours, then blend, strain, and aerate in a jug.

TIAN OF MUD CRAB, AVRUGA ROE AND YELLOW GAZPACHO FOAM

craft of all shapes and sizes snuggled into secluded bays and backwaters and others such as ourselves migrating north or south. Not long after midday we had reached the more open waters below Peel Island and set a course for Manly Boat Harbour where we took a berth at the Royal Queensland Yacht Squadron just as a strong wind warning was being issued. The winds and an electrical problem kept us here for a few days and we fell into the routine of a morning walk to the village to collect the papers and returning in the late afternoon to select a seafood dinner from the fishmonger's.

The Sheraton, Main Beach

Our Lady on the Sea

The Broadwater, Southport

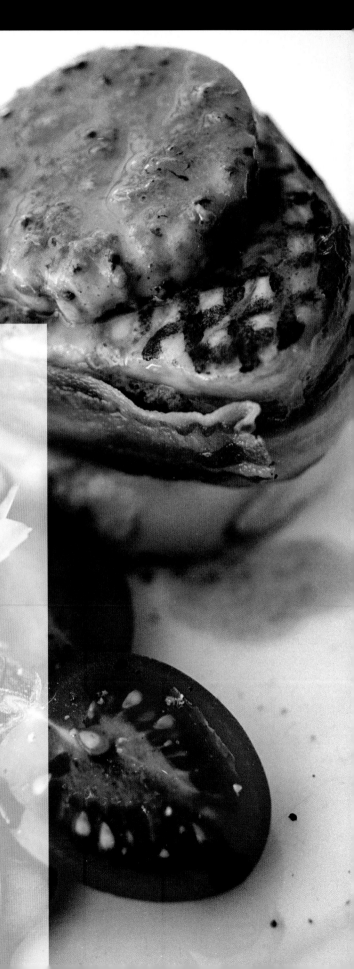

SEARED SWORDFISH MIGNON

PIER NINE

Back in 1991 Mathew Hill Smith bought Pier Nine and set about creating a wonderful, relaxing oasis in the middle of the corporate world and overlooking the meandering Brisbane River.

Mathew has always had culinary culture in his blood, being born into a wine making family at the forefront of Australia's wine industry for six generations.

Pier Nine has won numerous industry awards and is famous for its many varieties of freshly shucked natural oysters on the menu.

Rosemary's brother, Eugene, a resident of Brisbane tells us Pier Nine is one of his favourite places to relax and let the world roll by whilst relishing one of the delicious items on the menu with a glass of Shaw and Smith Sauvignon Blanc.

Preheat oven to 200c. Wrap 1 slice of pancetta around the outside of each swordfish steak and secure with a toothpick. Brush both sides with olive oil and sear each side for 2 minutes in a hot pan then continue to cook in the oven for a further 6 to 8 minutes. Remove and allow to rest.

Remove tooth picks, top with a slice of Café de Paris butter and serve on a mound of sweet potato with sweetheart tomato, basil and red onion salad.

To make a Café de Paris butter. Heat 2 tablespoons of butter in a small saucepan, add 1 finely chopped golden shallot and cook until translucent. Add 1 ½ teaspoons of paprika, a pinch of cayenne pepper, cook for a further minute. Stir in 1 tablespoon Worcestershire sauce, 1 tablespoon of tomato sauce, 1 tablespoon of seedless mustard. Boil until thickened and allow to cool.

In a separate bowl beat 150gm butter with 2 cloves finely chopped garlic, 1 teaspoon lemon juice, 1 anchovy fillet finely chopped. 1 cornichon finely chopped, 1½ teaspoons each of capers, parsley and chives all finely chopped, 1 egg yolk, salt and pepper. Combine with cooled mixture from above and form into a log, wrap in plastic and refrigerate until required.

Serve by removing toothpicks from pancetta and plate swordfish. Place a mound of dressed salad alongside then top fish with a slice of Café de Paris butter. Serves 6.

Hope Harbour

The southport fishing fleet

After a few days the wind eased and we set off for Mooloolaba by way of the anchorage at Tangalooma, where we spent a pleasant evening anchored off a sandy beach and barbecued on the aft deck with the loom of the mainland lights running for miles along the western sky. In the morning a steady south easterly followed us through the Spitfire and North West Channels across the top of Moreton Bay to Caloundra where the high rise on Point Cartwright was clearly visible on the northern horizon. On arriving off the normally reliable entrance to Mooloolaba we found a buoy marking an entrance confused by the build up of a new sand bar and after aborting our first approach waited to follow a local boat in.

Manly Marina, Moreton Bay

Caloundra Headland

Pumice Stone Passage separates Bribie Island from the mainland

Ricky Ricardo's sits on the north facing bank of the Noosa River and has a casual Mediterranean elegance and great views. Owned by well known Noosa personalities Leonie Palmer and Steven Fisher it is called after Steve's great uncle, Ricky, a lovable Irish raconteur and lover of poetry, fine cigars, music, good wine and beautiful women, all of which he could admire at Ricky Ricardo's today whilst savouring the fine food that his namesake is so famous for.

SEARED SCALLOPS ON TARO CRISPS

To make 24 pieces.

Peel, de-seed and finely shred 1 small very green and unripe papaya. In a heavy pan heat 2 tablespoons olive oil and saute 2 finely chopped golden shallots and 1 finely diced red chilli for 1 minute. Add papaya and cook over a high heat for 4-5 minutes. Add ¼ cup of sugar and ¼ cup fresh lime juice and cook for another 2 minutes. Spread on a tray and cool.

Add ½ bunch coriander finely chopped and ½ bunch Vietnamese mint finely chopped and mix.

Trim a 500gm piece of taro root and cut into 24 pieces 50mm square and 4mm thick and fry in hot oil until golden and crisp. Season with salt.

Cook the dried scallops quickly in a heavy pan. Place a teaspoon of papaya on 24 taro crisps and place a warm scallop on top. Sprinkle with sesame seeds, drizzle with extra virgin olive oil and serve immediately.

Mooloolaba

River frontages, Mooloola River, Mooloolaba

Prick 6 large ripe tomatoes all over with a fork and char grill until the skins are black and blistered. Cool, remove skins and blend. Season with 2 tablespoons of vinegar, 2 tablespoons sugar, salt and pepper and strain through a fine sieve.

Drain 1 cup of cannelloni beans that have been soaked overnight with 2 bay leaves, 2 cloves of garlic, sprigs of rosemary and thyme. Place in fresh cold water and bring to boil. Skim off any froth. Add 2 bay leaves, 2 cloves garlic, sprigs of rosemary and thyme, simmer for 45 minutes, adding some table salt towards the end. The beans should hold their shape but be soft and creamy. Drain, cool, remove the herbs and garlic.

Sweat 3 large red onions thinly sliced in a little olive oil until soft, add 2 tablespoons of vinegar and simmer for 5-10 minutes until absorbed, cool.

Mix together the beans, herbs, onion and 12 diced semi dried tomatoes and dress with extra virgin olive oil.

Dry the skin of 6 fillets of reef fish, sprinkle with salt and fry skin side down in a hot heavy pan until the skin is crispy. Turn and complete cooking.

To serve pour the consommé into 6 deep plates, arrange bean salad in the middle of each, place the fish on top.

CRISPED SKINNED REEF FISH FILLET

MOOLOOLABA TO HERVEY BAY.

Mike and Di Battle joined us at Mooloolaba and while waiting a few days for the weather to improve we renewed our acquaintance with this beautiful seaport and looked up our old neighbours from Hobart, Hedley and Judy Calvert and caught up with other friends. There is a substantial fishing fleet based here providing an abundance of fresh local seafood and we ate well at the restaurants along the banks of the Mooloola River. In due course the winds abated and after obtaining a promising report on the Wide Bay Bar from the Coast Guard at Tin Can Bay we headed off beneath a cloudless sky. Away to our port the long sandy beaches of the Sunshine Coast ran parallel to our course while seaward the perfect ocean stretched to the distant blue horizon. By lunch Noosa was well astern and the twin humps of Double Island Point clearly visible ahead. Our intention was to anchor behind Double Island Point and cross the Wide Bay Bar in the morning. A light north westerly had come in during the

Garry's Anchorage, a favourite stopover in the straits.

afternoon, not enough to make the anchorage untenable but it lived up to it's reputation as one of the most uncomfortable on the whole coast. Certainly we have always found it rough, beset by the dregs of the southeasterly swell that wraps round the point and invades the bay. However the discomfort is balanced by the bay's great beauty. We enjoyed the last of the light as it bathed the long sweep of the beach in a gentle glow and sparkled on the water, flecked white by schools of feeding tuna overflown by wheeling squadrons of raucous gulls. After a disturbed night we woke as the clear morning light played on the high cliffs of coloured sands lining the western shore and found the bay still alive with tuna. Eight nautical miles northward brought us to the leads to the Wide Bay Bar – a crossing we always face with some trepidation no matter what the conditions. It is a wide crossing; the first leg in through the channel with white water on both sides is a mile and a half long. Even in the prevailing calm conditions

Hervey Bay

at the top of the tide we found large swells standing up behind us and four or five times we surfed as they broke around us. The second leg of the entrance, running north parallel to Fraser Island and known locally as the 'mad mile', was also uncomfortable with the wind starting to play with the falling tide. Once inside the calm blue expanse of the Great Sandy Straits lay before us. On the seaward side Fraser Island, the largest sand island in the world, runs north for some forty miles while on the landward side are some small settlements, inlets and rivers running beyond the mangrove foreshores to the rich hinterland behind. We overnighted in a beautiful and calm anchorage at Tin Can Bay where we farewelled the Battles and woke in the morning to find a feast of sand crabs in our pot. Pushing northward at our normally leisurely pace we spent two nights in and around Gary's Anchorage where in the early mornings we watched dingoes patrolling the exposed shallows and during the day the passage of other craft as they headed north ahead of us or south from whence we had come. The next day we crossed the shallow 'hump' near Boonlye Point, where the waters drain north and south, and wound our way north through the channel markers to an anchorage off Woody Island at the entrance to Hervey Bay, arriving just before dusk. There was only one other yacht for company and no other sign of man other than a handful of distant riding lights on the Fraser Island shore.

MARINARA

Heat 250ml of olive oil in a dish. Cook prawns until the colour changes. Remove and add cubes of firm white fish and cook for a few minutes. Remove and cook squid rings for 2 minutes. Remove squid and mix in diced tomatoes, 3-4 cups of fish stock, add 1 cup of meat stock, a dash of saffron powder. Season with thyme, basil, salt and pepper to taste. Boil for 10 minutes then simmer (5 to 10 minutes). Add prawns, fish and squid. Serve with rice.

The golden XXXX Brand is the beer of choice for the vast majority of Queenslanders, and a fine drink it is, light and refreshing and not as dry as most of the southern brews - as befits the state that dominates Australian sugar production. The most important task each day for the 'bilge rat' was to ensure sufficient golden cans were properly chilled for happy hour. We also enjoyed some of the great wheat beers produced by the Eumundi Country Brewhouse located in the small picturesque township of Eumundi in the sunshine Coast hinterland. Brewed with fresh rain water and using the local sugar cane the lagers would satisfy the most discerning drinkers, not to mention thirsty sailors.

Around the Township of 1770

Cape Capricorn

The Bundaberg Distilling Company has been producing the best rum in Australia since 1889 and in their honour "bundies" were also a drink of choice for happy hours as we cruised the Capricorn Coast. Brewed from local sugar this smooth dark drink has an aroma and taste that is never forgotten and has the power to summon up memories from distant times and places. It is as good a companion in bleak and frozen mountains as it is in its tropical homeland and has sailed with sailors the world over since it became a staple in the British Navy centuries ago. Sugar is one of Queensland's major rural industries with extensive cane fields running from South East Queensland right through to Mossman in the north. Often at night the glow of burning cane fields marks the western horizon and is a reminder of the industry's hard and sometimes bitter past that has played such a part in defining the Australian character.

MARINATED
RED EMPEROR
SKEWERS

Red Emperor is one of the best of the tropical table fish and is great eating no matter how it is cooked. This is an easy way to enjoy it and enables the preparation to be done beforehand.

Cut 1kg of boneless Red Emperor or other firm fish in 2 cm cubes. Combine 3 cloves of crushed garlic, 2 teaspoons finely grated fresh ginger, ¼ teaspoon ground turmeric, ¼ cup of fish sauce, 2 tablespoons lime juice 1 teaspoon sugar, ¼ teaspoon dry chilli flakes and 1 tablespoon of olive oil. Add fish to marinade, mix well. Cover and refrigerate for 15 minutes. Thread fish and spring onions alternately onto 12 skewers. Cook skewers on a heated oiled grill or pan.

Serve skewers on steamed rice. Garnish with extra sliced spring onions and a quarter of a lemon.

Place 5 long red chillies, ½ Spanish onion, 3 cloves garlic, 1 tablespoon grated ginger, 2 tablespoons coriander, 1 tablespoon shrimp paste in food processor with a little oil to blend to a paste.

Move to pan and fry for a minute or two.

Add 1 large tin crushed tomatoes, 1 tablespoon oyster sauce, 2 stalks lemon grass, 2 tablespoons light soya sauce. Simmer for half an hour.

Add 2 -3 kgs Moreton Bay Bugs. Simmer 5 minutes or until cooked.

Serve on a bed of rice and drizzle sauce around the plate.

Mark and Rem, the previous owners of Oceania cooked this delicious dish for us on our arrival to Rosslyn Bay after a long passage. Sitting on their verandah sipping a glass of Chardonnay, (well maybe more than a glass) we caught up after quite a while, before they joined us on the trip further north on their yacht Knot Again.

Over the next few months we shared many wonderful meals cooked in the galleys of Knot Again and Oceania and some memorable barbecues on hot sandy beaches.

CHILLI BUGS

Great Keppel Island

HERVEY BAY TO 1770

The light southerlies and clear blue skies were still with us the next morning. Leaving our anchorage as a golden sun rose above Fraser Island, Oceania enjoyed a gentle reach towards our next port of call, Bundaberg Harbour at the mouth of the Burnett River. Through the translucent water the sandy bottom of Hervey Bay seemed close enough to touch as we cleared the fairway buoy and let the breeze fill our large genoa. Further out we spotted our first whales since Byron Bay and from time to time we were inspected by lone dolphins travelling at a gentle pace but not inclined to play in our wash as did their boisterous cousins further south. From time to time butterflies with their wings working busily were carried to us on the wind. Some paused for a moment but most flew casually past unconcerned that their next landfall was New Zealand. As the day passed the coastline began to draw closer again and nearing our destination the channel markers into the Burnett River rose out of the waters ahead. Entering the river we availed ourselves of the hospitality of the Bundaberg Port Marina, a new facility a short distance upstream. Later, as the cool night settled around us we ate fine local seafood at the 'Baltimore' the marina café overlooking the yachts and exchanged experiences with some of our fellow diners. We cast off our mooring lines in the last of the night's shadows and had cleared the markers and turned north before the sun rose. Once again our days run took us well out and the adjacent coast receded from view for some hours before the hills near Agnes Waters and the Township of 1770, so called to honour Cook's stopover so many years ago, peaked over the smooth blue horizon. Agnes Waters sits along a glorious set of beaches on the seaward side of Round Hill Head. Around the headland, on the northern side, a small creek runs to the ocean through sand banks and provides a delightful anchorage to boats with shallow enough draft to enter. Although previously we have risked the entrance it has generally been a near run thing and we decided to anchor outside in the bay. This is peaceful enough in a south easterly although the gentle swell that is never absent in any roadstead anchorage gave the yacht a restless night. Drinks on the aft deck beneath another beautiful sunset and later, in the gentle yellow glow of the hurricane lamp as darkness settled, we cooked marinated Red Emperor on skewers on the barbecue.

1770 TO ROSSLYN BAY.

In the morning we took the tender into the creek in search of memories and breakfast at the old general store and later motored the twelve miles to Pancake Creek. Secure and beautiful, easy to enter, lined by golden sandy beaches and tropical forest, this is one of the most loved anchorages on the whole of the Australian coast. We went ashore to swim and soak in the warm rock pools and in the evening dined on fresh sand crabs lightly baked in the shell and garnished with a white wine sauce. After a quiet night the morning sun brought back the light southeasterly and we set a course for Cape Capricorn some forty nautical miles to our north. Our course took us up the Curtis Channel passing some bulk carriers waiting to enter the port of Gladstone tucked inside Facing and Curtis Islands. By early afternoon we had anchored below the lighthouse on Cape Capricorn, a picturesque spot where we were sheltered from the southeasterly. Near by prawn trawlers were working close in around the rocky foreshore and later as the sun set behind the golden slopes of the cape our thoughts turned to the fresh banana prawns waiting in the galley for the chef's attention. For some days we had been listening to the very informative weather forecasts from 'Rocky Met' – the Australian Bureau of Meteorology office at

Rosslyn Bay Marina

Rockhampton and by early next morning it was growing more certain that we would shortly be in for a bout of strong winds generated by a large high over Bass Strait. It seemed like a good time to head for Rosslyn Bay Marina where we were to catch up with Mark and Rem Towers, the past owners of Oceania, who were planning to sail further north with us in their lovely Bavaria 42 'Knot Again'. Needing a making tide to clear the marina's entrance we delayed our departure until mid morning and with a cloudless sky and the southerly picking up the occasional white cap we ran across Keppel Bay under foresails and mizzen. The islands that dot the bay slid past one by one and by mid afternoon we were approaching Double Head and the marina tucked behind it. Mark and Rem were there to take our lines, and later sitting on their deck overlooking the marina we enjoyed a meal of fiery chillied Moreton Bay Bugs while making plans for what lay ahead. Overnight the winds built and by morning they were gusting thirty five to forty knots. We were pleased to be snugly secured and able to enjoy the friendly township of Yeppoon and this beautiful part of the coast including a trip to Great Keppel Island.

Great Keppel Island

Heat 100ml olive oil in large pan and add 2 tablespoons cumin and 1 tablespoon fennel seed. As they begin to pop add 2 sliced onions, 2 cloves crushed garlic, 2 tablespoons minced ginger, 1 stick celery, 2 bay leaves, ½ teaspoon turmeric and 1 tablespoon ground ginger. Fry over a high heat until the spices are fragrant and the onion begins to soften. Turn heat down, add 100 gm butter and sweat the mixture, stirring occasionally for 5-10 minutes.

Add 12 large very ripe tomatoes, skinned and diced, 1 cup cooked chickpeas, pinch saffron, and 1 litre of fish stock. Simmer until the tomatoes soften and become saucy. Season with salt and pepper.

When ready to serve, add 3 diced zucchini and cook for 2-3 minutes.

Add 24 large king prawns, peeled, (leave tail and preferably head intact) to the saucepan in a single layer, sprinkle with ½ cup black olives and cover with a lid.

Simmer gently in the sauce for 3-4 minutes until just cooked.

Garnish with 1 bunch of chopped coriander and serve with couscous.

Serves 4.

Recipe: Ricky Ricardo's Noosa

TAGINE OF PRAWNS, CHICKPEAS, ZUCCHINI & OLIVES

Pearl Bay

ROSSLYN BAY TO THE DUKE ISLANDS

The wind had finally abated when we followed 'Knot Again' out of the marina with the excited faces of Holly and Sasha, Mark and Rem's two Labradors, leaning over the deck. Dawn was breaking and outside an uncomfortable swell was still running, the sky sullen with patches of low cloud trailing misty tendrils of rain. Great Keppel and North Keppel Islands were grey shadows on the horizon, sometimes lost to sight behind the curtains of passing showers. The making tide generated a strong northward set and we bowled along at a good pace and by the time we had cleared Cape Manifold the sky was clearing and the sun beginning to sparkle on the tumbling waves. However despite their beauty the waters around the Cape

Patterns on the beach at Pearl Bay

can be treacherous with the strong currents creating dangerous eddies and over falls. In the warmer months localised thunderstorms can develop with surprising speed and a peaceful afternoon transformed to a dark maelstrom in a matter of minutes. On a previous passage calm seas had lulled us into towing a quite large aluminium dinghy rather than stowing it on deck, which was our normal custom. Before we had appreciated what was happening a dark thunderhead formed and began to march on us hurling forty-knot gusts as it came. The sea, which only minutes before had been placid, was a jumble of breaking waves as the wind fought against the tide and before we could do a thing the dinghy was capsized, its doubled painters snapped and it was last seen half afloat being driven towards the beach. But today we were confronted with no such calamity and by the time

Beautiful Pearl Bay

Melt 50gms of margarine in pan. Add one diced onion stirring until soft. Add 2 tablespoons flour. Cook, stirring until grainy. Stir in 375ml of light creamy evaporated milk combined with 1 cup of water. Stir until mixture boils and thickens. Simmer for 3 minutes. Add 650gm of seafood marinara mix (or any firm fish) and grated lemon rind. Cook whilst stirring for approximately 3 minutes. Stir in ½ a cup of grated cheese and a sprig of dill. Divide mixture between four small ovenproof dishes; sprinkle with a further half a cup of cheese and half a cup of stale bread crumbs. Cook under a hot grill for about 6 minutes or until golden brown. Garnish with a sprig of dill.

MIXED SEAFOOD MORNAY

Joe and Liz Brischetto produce a number of fine wines at their vineyard near Bargara a beautiful spot on the coast a few miles south of Burnett Heads. Whether travelling by boat and staying over in the Burnett River, or by road, we always try to pay a visit. Not only for the wine but also for the cheerful Sicilian hospitality. Joe now produces a mellow shiraz, a Coral Coast Sweet Red, a shiraz Cabernet Sauvignon, a Merlot, a Chardonnay and a White Muscat as well as some ports. Watching the sun set we sipped an aperatif of white muscat and later as the stars blazed brilliantly over Pearl Bay we enjoyed a crisp fruity chardonnay with our seafood mornay.

we were passing the wide entrance to Port Clinton and approaching our destination at Pearl Bay it was a beautiful afternoon. The rocky coastline, broken by small bays and islands clothed in Norfolk Pines, was bathed in a golden light. The water was a patchwork of translucent blues and greens and the breaks along the reefs and cliff faces the purest white. Pearl Bay is protected by heavily timbered hills that rise steeply behind the crescent of its white beach and a cluster of small islands that lie a few hundred meters off shore. We anchored on a sandy bottom in five meters of crystal clear water and let the beauty of the bay wash over us. So beautiful in its enchantment, that for this time at least, no more could be asked of life. The afternoon drifted into night and the golden crescent of a waning moon hung suspended above the dark hills. Overhead the night sky blazed and the only sound that reached us was the gentlest wash of the waves on shore. In the morning we followed the sweep of Pearl Bay north, staying close inshore to appreciate the string of small golden beaches that each lie within their own headlands. Each one is perfect, but each seemingly more beautiful than the last. By midday we had anchored in Island Head Creek, a large sandy estuary that is secure in all weather, and spent the afternoon ashore walking along the ocean beach that leads to Pine Trees Point. The coast here is still an eye-catching mixture of beaches, headlands and rocky islets. Thick tropical forest, mixed with stands of paper barks and casuarinas line the beaches framed between dramatic green headlands decorated with stands of Norfolk Island pines. Some other yachts came in during the afternoon and in the dusk we could pick out their riding lights tucked well up in the small bays protected by drying banks of sand. Our path the next day took us around Townshend Island and across the mouth of

Island Head

Shoalwater Bay to Hunter Island, part of the Duke Isles, forty miles to the north. The weather was still idyllic with a calm sea and just enough wind to fill our sails. The huge tides along this part of coast produce strong currents and we found ourselves assisted by a two knots set. Having passed some more southerly islands on the way we were anchored off the south west point of Hunter Island by early afternoon. There are four or five main islands and any number of islets in the Dukes and in the light conditions we could have chosen any number of delightful anchorages, and gained protection in most weather.

THE DUKE ISLANDS TO LAGUNA KEYS

Oceania rested quietly during the night, the only movement her gentle swing to the change of tide and in the morning we awoke to find the distant mainland a grey stripe against the clear pale sky. As the sun rose the colours ripened and by the time we weighed anchor the sea stretched rich blue to the curved horizon. So still it seemed a painted canvas that, if we so chose, we could have easily strolled upon. We motored up the narrow channel between Hunter and Marble islands and after clearing the close shoals laid a course for Middle Percy Island some twenty miles to the north east. The water remained unruffled by any wind and when anchored in West Bay, a place renowned for its roll, we found it as still as could be desired.

WARM SCALLOP SALAD

Marinate scallops in a marinade of lemon and garlic for 10 minutes.

In a saucepan toast a pinch of saffron for a few seconds, add 1 finely chopped onion, finely diced zest of 2 lemons and cook for 30 seconds. Add 100ml tomato juice, 100ml white balsamic vinegar, 125ml extra virgin olive oil, simmer for 10 minutes, add juice of 1 lemon. Set aside.

Blanch 3 Roma tomatoes, refresh, peel, discard the seeds and dice the remainder. Quarter 3 bulbs of baby fennel, add olive oil, two cloves finely diced garlic, season, sear for 2-3 minutes. Set aside.

Cook scallops for 30 seconds each side in a hot pan Add chopped tomatoes and herbs to the dressing. Serve by arranging scallops around the fennel and spooning the dressing over the fennel and drizzle around the plate.

Recipe: Riva on the Noosa River at Noosa, where you can arrive by ferry and bask on the sun soaked deck, serenaded by the gentle lapping of the blue waters below.

RIVA

The Mount Uncle Distillery is situated in the fertile Atherton Tablelands, amongst orchards of avocados, macadamian nuts, limes, bananas and mangoes. Using centuries old techniques the 'Calli' Limecello captures the beauty and the smooth tang of fresh limes and encapsulates the zest of the lime peel in a traditional Italian style. Served chilled it is a refreshing drink with a dry crisp palate and is wonderful between courses or as an aperitif and is peculiarly well suited to languid tropical nights.

The Duke Isles

Middle Percy Island

LINGUINE WITH PESTO AND PRAWNS

Spread 25gm of pine nuts on a baking sheet in an oven preheated to 165c and toast for 6 minutes until slightly browned. Set aside. Add 350gm tiger prawns to a large pan filled with boiling water, cook for 2 minutes, remove with a slotted spoon, dip in cold water and let cool. Pull off the tails, shell and remove the intestinal tract. Cook 180gm of dried linguine till tender, drain and keep warm. During the time the pasta is cooking warm a dash of olive oil in a small pan, add 1 clove of crushed garlic. After 5 minutes add prawns, pine nuts, 20gm of basil and a squeeze of lemon juice. Mix and pour onto pasta, season with salt and pepper and toss.

Divide into 4 portions, sprinkle with grated Parmesan cheese. Serve with salad.

West Bay, Middle Percy

The palm trees lining the beach stood motionless above the shining sand and the line of the falling tide was unbroken by any surge. We spent the last of the golden afternoon ashore, idling in the warm water and inspecting the famous mariners' hut rich with mementos of passing yachts. Later we barbecued banana prawns under the light of the hurricane lamp and watched the slow rotation of the sky above us. For the last few days we had been watching the progress of a strong high-pressure system crossing the Great Australian Bight and the evening weather report from the Mackay Met Bureau indicated that the winds would build to gale force over the next few days. This, and an approaching rendezvous with Rob's brother Richard and his wife Franny at Laguna Keys, decided us to push on north rather than idle around the Percys, which had been our intention. The rising sun saw us well clear of the Percys running before a gentle south easterly and as it built to a balmy ten knots we watched Digby Island with its picturesque crater like anchorage slide by. By the time we were abeam of Prudhoe Island the distant hump of St. Bees Island, our destination sixty odd miles north of the Percys, had risen above the horizon and an hour before sundown we were snugly anchored in the narrow Egremont Passage

that separates St. Bees from its twin, Keswick Island. Although we had anchored as close as prudent to the fringing reef we were still quite a distance, four or five hundred meters, from the dense tropical forest along the foreshore and we were amazed at the cacophony of bird calls that floated out to us. They reached a crescendo in the dusk but dropped away once darkness had settled and the wind built, which working against the strong tidal flow in the passage gave us a somewhat disturbed night. The southerlies remained moderate during our passage up the Hillsborough Channel to Repulse Bay and the marina at Laguna Keys and at 3pm we arrived, delighted to find Richard and Franny waiting to take our lines.

Cruising past Brampton Island

Langford Reef and Hook Island, "The Whitsundays"

whitsundays to townsville

scuba diving, Whitsunday Islands

LAGUNA KEYS TO BOWEN

Strong winds kept us in port for the duration of Richard and Franny's stay and it was not until they had returned to the southern winter that a moderate system re-established itself. Even then, after a trip back to Hobart to catch up with family and business, we had to beat out of Repulse Bay against 25 knots. The Whitsunday Passage was running an uncomfortable sea that sent sheets of spray flying across our decks as we followed 'Knot Again' towards the beautiful anchorage in the western bay of Thomas Island. On board were Max and Viv Doerner, now fellow Tasmanians and in times past friends from Rob's school years in Manly and Peter Langford an old army friend now living in Canberra, together with a friend of his another Viv. In mid afternoon we reached Thomas with its lagoon like bay fringed by three small beaches separated by rocky bluffs and protected to the north by a rocky islet. The bay was ours alone and we anchored close in to the centre beach to avoid the swell that somehow crept in and the occasional bullets of wind that swept down from the crown of the island. Over the next two days the wind eased and we spent our days relaxing on the beaches, swimming in the shallow warm waters and cooking around a fire piled with aromatic driftwood. The nights were dark with only a sliver of new moon. But above us the universe was ablaze and out to the east Mars shone like the riding light, a great phantom galleon. With a fairly tight schedule to Bowen and the prospect of rising winds we opted to sail north along the passage inside Long and Molle Islands to Woodwark Bay, rather than the more familiar route via Lindeman and Whitsunday Islands. After a wonderful thirty mile run with a fifteen knot south easterly behind us we rounded Grimston Point as the wind began to pick up, whipping spray from the breaking white caps, and we were happy to slip into the calm waters at the head of the bay. The coastline ahead of us was indented with numerous bays

A coral garden, Great Barrier Reef

SWEET CHILLI PRAWNS WITH SNOW PEAS

Heat 100ml of olive oil, finely shredded kaffir lime leaves, crushed garlic, grated ginger and cook until sizzling. Add diced capsicum, onion, sweet soy sauce, chilli sauce and stir for 2-3 minutes. Add green prawns, coriander, chopped baby chillies, snow peas, salt and pepper to taste and stir until prawns are cooked through.

Serve with steamed jasmine rice.

offering protection from the southerly trade winds and with strong winds forecast for the next few days we decided to move a few miles to a small, unnamed bay opposite Grassy Island. Here we found a sheltered beach that could be approached through a channel in the fringing coral reef and while some idled on the coral sand Peter trolled along the reef's face and was finally rewarded with a good sized trevally. In the late afternoon we set a crab pot off a patch of mangroves and then retired to the comfort of the saloon to enjoy battered fillets of trevally while the wind continued to pipe in at over twenty knots. Beyond this anchorage the coast continued to run away to the northwest before turning west through the majestic Gloucester Passage. A number of steep rocky islets dotted the offshore waters before the great bulk of Gloucester Island, crowned by the high peak of Mount Bertha, became visible behind George Point. Inland, the precipitous coastal ranges marched close to the shore, dense patches of rain forest standing amid rocky crags. White caps chased us northwards; gulls wheeled overhead while a pair of sea eagles patrolled the rocky foreshore. Rounding George Point we found some protection from the boisterous winds and before long we glided into the calm waters of the Gloucester Channel. We joined a number of other yachts anchored off the beach south of Passage Islet and went ashore to enjoy a drink at Monty's, a low-key resort towards the western end of the passage. Afterwards we lay in the warm shimmering water lapping the gently shelving beach and returned to Oceania at sunset, salty and sun kissed, to enjoy barramundi with a green curry sauce, courtesy of the crew of 'Knot Again'. In the morning we had a great run across Edgecumbe Bay with a stiff southeasterly blowing off the shore and within two hours we were manoeuvring in the crowded confines of Bowen Boat Harbour. Max and Viv were leaving us here and it was sad to unload them on the fuel jetty along with mountains of diving and golf gear (Max is not one to pass up the chance of a round on a new course, and Laguna Keys is one of the best). We were cheered by the usual good humour of the fishermen readying themselves for the days work and by being able to take on board a good supply of fresh prawns and mud crabs. After topping up with fuel and water we motored round to Greys Bay where we anchored well out and baked the crabs in the barbecue.

BOWEN TO TOWNSVILLE

Cape Upstart, named by Captain Cook in recognition of its dominance of the surrounding low lying coast, is forty nautical miles northwest of Bowen. It is a secure and beautiful stopover with a number of anchorages off small white beaches dominated by towering granite buttresses or in the protected waters of Nobbies

Bananas are grown commercially from the northern NSW coast to the Cairns region in tropical Far North Queensland. The Mount Uncle Distillery in the Atherton Tablelands makes a fine Banana Liqueur, the Elixir de Musa, which is the base of a number of tropical cocktails that are appropriate for the light hearted atmosphere of the Whitsundays. Try a Monsoon 'Mudslide'. 15mls Banana Liqueur, 15mls Vodka, 15mls Kahlua, 15mls Baileys Irish Cream, 30mls Creams, 30mls milk, 1 Banana. Blend with ice until smooth. Alternatively sip the liqueur under a star filled tropical sky while listening to the rhythm of the rumba.

These remote 'getaways' at Cape Upstart are only accessible by water.

One of several anchorages behind the high bulk of Cape Upstart

Inlet and Cape Creek. Ashore there is a scattering of houses that have been laboriously built by carting materials solely by sea, as there is no road connection. We spent a number of days here swimming and cooking ashore at our choice of deserted beach. Even in strong winds that sometimes produced 'bullets' of thirty knots and more there was always a protected spot ashore where we could laze under the lee of some massive boulder lying at the waters edge. The water was warm and clear and the course grain sand of the beaches untrodden. Our next stop, Cape Bowling Green, could hardly be more different. A long low sand spit projecting into a shallow bay and orientated so as to give very little protection from the prevailing south easterlies and none from the north. Definitely a fine weather stopover only and after a restless night we were up and away early, glad to escape from the annoying swell that sweeps into the bay and on our way to Townsville. After a pleasant day's sail we rounded Cape Cleveland and motored over the wide shallow expanse of Cleveland Bay to catch the high tide through the shallow channel into Townsville's fine Breakwater Marina. A popular, busy harbour where we were only able to secure a berth for a seven-day stopover. Here we bade farewell to Peter and Viv and a few days later welcomed Sue and Don Clark back on board. Townsville has recently undergone great changes and with a relatively dry climate is now a very desirable yachting destination. The waterfront has been transformed by the leafy greenness of The Strand, the city's fine old buildings are showcased to present very attractive streetscapes and there is a plethora of fine restaurants offering a wide choice of style and excellent local seafood and beef.

townsville to cairns

MICHELE'S

Tied up to the marina in Townsville we ambled up to Palmer Street and found Michele's. Here with Mark, Rem Sue and Don we enjoyed one of the best meals of our trip. In fact it was so good we went back a second time.

Rosti: Place 1 large baking potato, peeled and grated in a clean cloth and squeeze away excess water. Place in bowl and season with salt and pepper and one tablespoon of melted butter. Form potato into round discs. Heat olive oil and butter in a heavy pan and fry rosti on both sides untill brown.

Bugs: Season 8 medium bugs and fry with butter untill cooked. Flambé in brandy, then remove from pan to plate. Use same pan to fry bug shells until bright in colour; add 1 glass white wine and 600mls beef stock and reduce by half. Remove shells and wash with water. Strain sauce and keep warm.

Beef: Pre-heat oven to 200c. Using sharp knife make an opening in 4 pieces of eye fillet 4-5cm thick. Lightly coat bug meat with 50gm garlic butter and insert in fillet opening. Heat 50mls of olive oil and 50gm butter in pan and sear steak for one minute each side. Bake in oven for 8 minutes. Remove and flambé in brandy.

To serve: Cut each fillet in two and serve on rosti potato. Decorate the plate with the bug shell. Spoon over sauce and serve with vegetables of your choice. Garnish with fresh herbs and a lime wedge.

ROSTI FILLET OF BEEF WITH FRESH MORETON BAY BUGS

Townsville and Magnetic Island fore shores and Bedarra Island

Magnetic Island

Townsville Marina and Castle Hill

TOWNSVILLE TO PORT HINCHINBROOK.

As with most of the islands in this stretch of the Queensland coast Magnetic Island is a bold and beautiful island with rocky tree covered slopes rising dramatically from the sea and sheltering a number of small beaches and anchorages. We anchored in Horseshoe Bay around midday, tucking as far as possible into the south-eastern corner where excellent shelter was available. The next morning we set off in the dinghy to explore the small settlement we could glimpse half hidden behind the palms fringing the beach. As we motored slowly through our neighbouring yachts we passed a flotilla of sea kayaks headed towards White Lady Bay, a small strip of sand near the northern point. Ashore the atmosphere was relaxed and casual. A number of more senior travellers like ourselves but far many more youthful backpackers from seemingly every corner of the world, all with happy faces and ready smiles. Though most of the island is national park it still supports a vibrant community, a mixture of Townsville commuters, those who have dropped out in paradise and others servicing a busy tourist industry. Across the shimmering water of Cleveland Bay lay Townsville; sitting below the great rocky crag called Castle Hill, forever changing its hues as the sun plays across its face. Leaving Magnetic we cavorted north, running before the reliable south easterlies that had built up a swell of a meter or so and flecked the waters of Halifax Bay with white caps. By midday we had entered Steamer Passage that runs between Great Palm Island, covered in rain forest and dominated by the cloud-covered peak of Mount Bentley,

Horseshoe Bay, Magnetic Island

Sunset at Pioneer Bay, Orpheus Island

and a cluster of smaller islands with white sandy beaches and fringing reefs. Two hours later we had dropped the anchor in Little Pioneer Bay at the northern end of Orpheus Island. To our north the great mountains of Hinchinbrook Island lined the horizon while at the head of our bay a small beach was framed by the luminous green of the mangroves edging the shore. After a walk on the beach we enjoyed a peaceful twilight on the aft deck, the soft light of the hurricane light enveloping us in a golden glow and the aroma of Barramundi and crusted cheese drifting deliciously from the barbecue. In the morning we passed through the shallow approaches to Hinchinbrook Channel, our eyes seldom off the depth sounder, which showed less than a meter under the keel for quite some distance. Once inside the island there is plenty of water provided you keep to the channel, so paying close attention to the channel markers we motored through the placid waters, alive with reflections of the mainland ranges and the nearer massifs of the island. We anchored inside Haycock Island, perfectly protected by the island and the projection of Reis Point. It was an anchorage of overwhelming beauty. The high mountains with mist covered peaks, dramatic lichen covered rock faces, ridges and valleys of impenetrable rainforest, placid winding waterways lined with the latticework of mangrove roots; all encompassed within a mantle of fragile serenity. In the still darkness Mars shone again with an unnatural radiance, and in the quiet of the next morning, while the sun still hung below the mountains, the whole scene was perfectly inverted in the mirror of the channel. We lingered here, reluctant to break the spell, but also needing a high tide to enter Port Hinchinbrook where we were to stop over for some mechanical repairs.

Orpheus Island

PORT HINCHINBROOK TO CAIRNS

Port Hinchinbrook is a man made harbour cut into the mainland shore of the Hinchinbrook Channel towards its northern end, just below the sleepy village of Cardwell. It is a pretty place with fine views, a friendly atmosphere and a restaurant overlooking the marina that proved popular with the crew for dinners and breakfasts. After an enjoyable few days we left on an evening high tide to cross the channel and anchor near the beach under Scraggy Point. Another magical anchorage with the backdrop of the high mountains, veiled with mist broken by streams of late golden sun. Later Mars climbed above Mount Pitt and hung brightly above its dark mass waiting for the silver crescent of the moon to cast its ghostly light along the still waters of the channel. In the morning we weighed anchor for Dunk Island, promising ourselves a longer visit to this beautiful area we had spent far too brief a time in. There was not a zephyr as we motored clear of Hecate Point on the northern extremity of the channel then past Goold

Dredging the entrance to Hinchinbrook Harbour

Island, an attractive high standing island off to our starboard. Later as we approached Dunk Island a north-easterly sea breeze began to build and by the time we arrived it was strong enough to make us seek protection off the southern shore where the shelving water forced us to anchor well out. The casual beach-side bistro on Dunk welcomes day visitors and passing yachts and is a delightful spot to pass some time with a drink or a game of pool or chess. Further around the main resort is hidden within tropical gardens spilling onto a sandy beach and a track leads to the top of the rainforest covered hills that dominate the island. What had seemed a sea breeze had by evening built into a steady twenty knot northerly and it was quite rolley as we entertained the crew of Knot Again and dined on a mackerel that Don had landed on the way across, baked with herbs and spices. Delicious. Next morning the wind was still against us so we spent the day exploring more of the island and retrieving the crab pot, which despite our usual high expectations yielded nothing. Forced to dine on fillets of mackerel. Oh well, life can be difficult. We left for Mourilyan Harbour the

CRABS

Crabbing, using a drum shaped crab pot made of netting which allows crabs easy access through apertures, but no escape once inside, was always a popular pastime amongst the crew. We started crabbing in earnest in the Southport Broadwater, where Blue Swimmers were plentiful, and had more success in the Great Sandy Straits but a somewhat mixed result for 'Muddies', the Queensland Mud Crab, thereafter. Most would agree that there is no finer seafood, best cooked by boiling and eaten (with rolled up sleeves and large pliers) chilled with a light dressing.

Bush Cherry wine is made from the fruit of the Cedar Bay or Beech Cherry, a sweet tasting native fruit similar in appearance to the introduced species. The wine itself is not unlike a nutty sherry and we found it a very pleasant aperitif, (in balmy tropical evenings, best drunk chilled) as well as being a fine accompaniment to a spicy meal.

Sizzle olive oil and crushed garlic for 2-3 minutes. Add a dash of lemon. Dip fish fillets in whisked egg, roll in grated Parmesan cheese and cook for around 3 minutes on each side and the crust is golden brown.

REEF FISH IN GARLIC PARMESAN CRUST

The lychee has been grown in China for centuries and was probably introduced to Australia by Chinese gold seekers in the 1870's. In doing so they were part of the tradition that has continued to enrich our cuisine from the time of the first fleet onwards. De Brueys Wines, a short distance beyond Kuranda, produces a fine lychee wine with fresh overtones of the lychee and rich tropical fruit aromas.

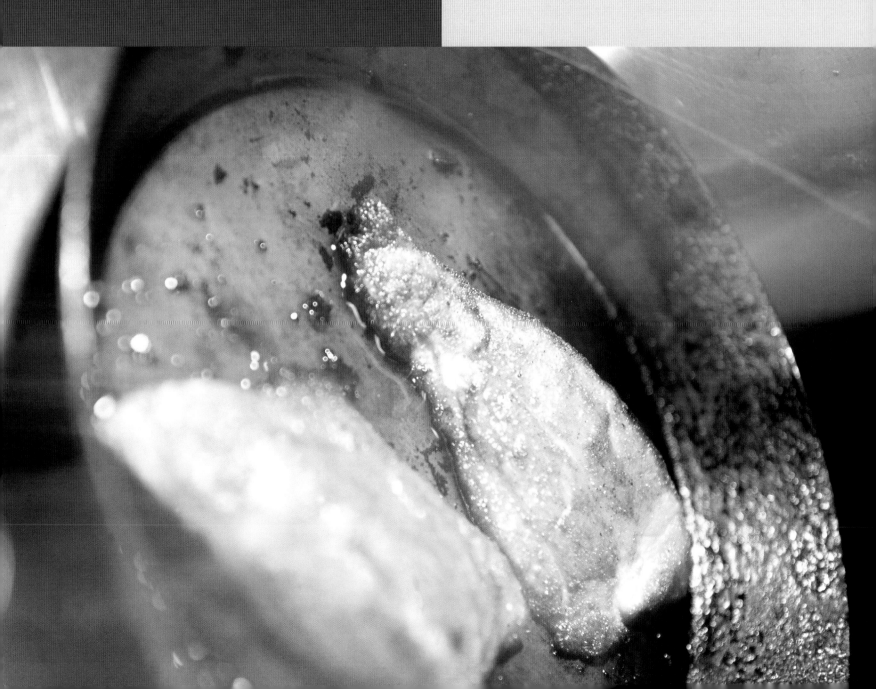

The stunning anchorage at Haycock Island, Hinchinbrook Channel

Port Hinchinbrook

Dunk Island

following morning, idling along before a ten-knot south-easterly that continued to ease as the day warmed. There was nothing left by lunchtime when we motored through the deep channel, past the high-forested hills standing at the entrance, into the totally enclosed harbour. Inside we found a collection of prawn trawlers waiting out the daylight hours and a few yachts and cruisers strung between pile berths. We pulled our anchor well into the muddy bottom feeling as secure as is possible on an anchor. However the change of tide dragged a trawler down on us and over our anchor chain. Unable to move or to waken the slumbering crew a collision seemed imminent, but at the last moment a tousled fisherman appeared and calamity was averted. The mangrove covered shore looked ideal for crabs so the pot was set, well baited with fish heads, and we retired to the aft deck confident that a good haul was imminent. But the dawn saw our hopes dashed again, and beneath the scornful eyes of our wive's we motored out the channel and turned north for Fitzroy Island, arriving in the early afternoon. Fitzroy is only a few miles from Cairns and supports a resort popular with the backpackers who flock there to soak up winter sun and to visit the reefs, which here are only a few miles off shore. We enjoyed the atmosphere for a couple of days, eating beside the pool and climbing the steep track over the island's hump to the lighthouse. In due course we left for Cairns, passing beautiful Turtle Bay and a little later the large expanse of Mission Bay before entering the channel into Cairns Harbour.

Fitzroy Island

From the heights of Fitzroy Island with Cairns lost in the blue beyond.

Off Port Douglas

cairns to thursday island

'Blue Lagoon' Cairns

There are many fine places to dine in Cairns - either right on the waterfront or in the adjacent vibrant city fringes, generally swinging to the beat of the backpackers out to make every moment count. Ian Candy, one of Cairns best known chefs, prepared this delicious dish for us. Mahi Mahi is a fish he has found combines well with spicy flavours.

To prepare the pepitas: lightly cook the following in a wok: I cup of pepitas, ½ cup virgin olive oil, 3 cloves chopped garlic, I chilli, 3 tablespoons ground cummin, I chopped white onion. Add coriander leaves to taste and blend.

Boil sweet potato, blanch fresh green beans, grill pieces of chorizo, and serve with char grilled mahi mahi spread with the pepita blend.

CHAR GRILLED MAHI MAHI WITH PEPITA

Strong winds were forecast and had started to chop up the water as we entered the new Marlin Marina at Cairns. We were glad to be there before they became a problem for us, but even as it was we managed to make a hash of docking anyway. Although we had a 'blow on' berth, one where the wind is supposed to gently lay you alongside, the tide pulling us away proved stronger and we had to scramble with lines and a winch to pull ourselves in. For a change the crew were supportive of the helmsman, muttering how deceptive tidal flows can be in unfamiliar situations and how a bystander had dropped the bowline. We had not been in Cairns for a few years and were pleasantly surprised by the improvements to the Marina and boardwalk areas and the addition of a picturesque 'lagoon' that attracted hordes of beautiful young things sunning themselves and speaking in many tongues. There was excellent eating within an easy walk and we enjoyed fresh local seafood or Italian, Thai and Indian cuisine before strolling home in the balmy evenings, the waterfront still vibrant and filled with music and laughter. Behind the city the dim outline of the high coastal mountains embraced us, to seaward the lights of yachts twinkled on the dark water. In no time at all the day of Don and Sue's departure arrived and we were farewelling them for a before dawn departure from Cairns airport. A few days later, on an almost perfect day, we made the short hop to Port Douglas, one of our very favourite places. Although it is a popular destination world wide 'The Port' still retains much of the charm of what it was, a simple fishing village. Although popularity has had some costs it has added a vibrancy and fine dining. There are a handful of world-class restaurants, many not far behind them and good simple fare is available at the pubs, yacht or combined clubs at very reasonable prices. For a yacht the Marina Mirage is handy to everything and from the aft deck we enjoyed a fine view over Dickson Inlet to the mountains beyond. Just as important there was a slipway handy that could lift out our spruce mast and make some repairs that had worried us since Laguna Keys. While this was underway we enjoyed the charms of the Port and caught up with a number of old friends. Before long we were saddly waiving off Mark and Rem on Knot Again as they hoisted their sails and headed south to their home port at Rosslyn Bay. While work continued on the mast we made preparations for the next leg of our voyage, aboard the MV Trinity Bay, which was to take us the Thursday Island and back.

'The Wharf' Port Douglas

PORT DOUGLAS TO THURSDAY ISLAND.

The Trinity Bay is a steel passenger and cargo vessel of 1594 tonnes that runs a weekly service from Cairns to Thursday Island and return. It is the lifeline of the coastal settlements north of Cooktown and in the Torres Straight Islands and the fishing fleets operating there. Everything they require other than airfreightable items must be carried north in her bulging holds; this includes all meats and vegetables, groceries, diesel, LPG, machinery, building supplies, including even sand and gravel. We sailed from Cairns in the late afternoon and twilight saw us enjoying the cool breeze on the

Four Mile Beach from Flagstaff hill.

On the Inlet is a Port Douglas institution popular with both visitors and locals because of its fine food and magnificent situation - actually built out over Dickson Inlet. Here you can watch the boat traffic come and go and admire memorable sunsets over the ranges. On a balmy tropical night, surrounded by the soft light of candles it has the essence of the far north. With Oceania tied up at the Marina Mirage this is where we celebrated Rob's birthday with friends.

To prepare the Salsa dice and combine the following ingredients to taste. 4 de seeded Roma tomatoes, 100gm of Persian fetta, 1 red onion, 8 basil leaves, 100gm kalamatta olive halves, 100ml extra virgin olive oil, 100gm baby capers, juice of 1 lemon, salt and pepper. Prepare a mash of 4 potatoes, 50gm of kalamatta olives, 50gm of butter, salt, pepper and nutmeg to taste. Prepare a balsamic glaze from 250ml balsamic vinegar and ½ cup of white sugar simmered until reduced by 25%.

Char grill the tuna to taste, serve on the mash and top with the salsa. Serve with asparagus spears and a slice of baked prosciutto.

ON THE INLET

CHAR GRILLED YELLOW FIN WITH PERSIAN SALSA

The Lady Douglas, serene in Dickson Inlet

The Daintree meets the Reef

PEPPERS BLOOMFIELD

If you are looking for a touch of indulgence and to get away from it all. Peppers Bloomfield is an exclusive secluded far north Queensland tropical hide-away only accessible by plane or boat. Tucked into the rainforest beneath a small headland beside a white tropical beach it is as far away from the everyday as you could find.

Arrange radicchio leaves as a bed on a plate. Cook sufficient cous cous, mix the flesh of limes through and season to taste, and add to the radicchio leaves. Puree mango, lime zest and sugar syrup to taste. Pan fry barramundi, place on top of the cous cous, pour on the mango syrup and garnish with a lemon wedge.

PAN FRIED BARRAMUNDI AND MANGO

Looking west from the tip of Cape York, the northern most part of mainland Australia

aft deck, and by the time darkness settled we were off Port Douglas. During the night we passed Endeavour Reef, which on a night such as this in 1770 had come so close to ending Cook's voyage in disaster. Shortly afterwards the lights of Cooktown, where the Endeavour was careened and repaired, lay sprinkled along the dark coastal ridges and later we passed Lizard Island, off to our starboard. At dawn we were off Cape Melville, the rising sun playing on the amazing piles of boulders, playthings of the gods heaped so carelessly there. The sun climbed higher above an azure sea glittering with silver and flecked with whitecaps. Around us lay the pale outlines of sunken reefs fringed by the white wash of breaking waves, golden cays and islets laced with tossing palms. The glory of the scene takes your breath and belies the dangers of sailing this most beautiful of coastlines. In 1889 Mahina, the most violent hurricane on record, with murderous winds and an almost incomprehensible tidal surge of over 12 meters, took 307 lives and 59 vessels in nearby Princess Charlotte Bay. In the afternoon the Trinity Bay paused to unload stores for the community at Lockhart

Aboard the MV Trinity Bay

The MV Trinity Bay returning via The Albany Passage

River and afterwards passed Restoration Island, Captain Bligh's first landfall after the mutiny on the Bounty and his extraordinary cruise in the ship's long boat. The south-easterly continued to pipe in at a steady twenty knots and over to the east we could occasionally pick up the spray of the swell crashing on the outer reefs. On the mainland a number of trawlers were sheltering in the secure anchorage at Portland Roads, the stepping off point for many allied servicemen leaving for the New Guinea campaign in World War 11. Once again the sun slipped behind the coastal ranges leaving the low clouds bathed in crimson and gradually darkness crept over us and we were left with our thoughts. Of Cook and Bligh and the men who had sailed with them and of the young men who had sailed north so many years later to give their lives for a nation these great navigators had helped create. The islands of the reef continued to slide past, some mere shadows, others marked by a lighthouse or the dim lights

Lizard Island is a work of nature's art right on the Barrier Reef and with twenty four glorious white sandy beaches to enjoy. Secluded and exclusive it is paradise.

Sitting on the verandah at Osprey's restaurant which overlooks the beach and ocean beyond it is difficult to imagine one has a worry in the world. Each day the menu changes and as the emphasis is on seafood the delights are many.

Mix together 400gm of smoked salmon together with 6 opal basil, 6 green Thai basil, 4 Vietnamese mint, 4 spearmint and 13 coriander leaves.

Pound 4 red chillies, 5 shallots, 4 garlic cloves, 6 coriander roots into a paste in a mortar and pestle, pound in 60gm palm sugar. Mix with lime juice and 150ml of fish sauce.

To serve: Place wasabi leaves in the centre of the plate. Mix together the smoked salmon, herbs and dressing and place into the centre of the leaf. Garnish with salmon caviar, crispy fried garlic, fresh chilli and shallots.
Serves 4.

LIZARD ISLAND

WASABI LEAF, HOUSE-SMOKED SALMON, CAVIAR AND THAI HERB SALAD

We had enjoyed the wines from Barambah Ridge Winery throughout our trip up the Queensland Coast and had brought with us a few bottles to toast 'journeys end'. The winery is located in a picturesque valley in the South Burnett Region and produces an excellent range of wines with some Hunter Valley characteristics as well as their own individuality. Their unwooded big warm climate chardonnays, full bodied with good aromas of melon and stone fruits have an elegant palate.

To poach salmon - add 3 cups virgin olive oil and 3 cups duck fat together and place in a baking dish. Add 800 gm fresh salmon, 3 sprigs thyme and 3 sprigs rosemary. Sprinkle sea salt . With salmon completely covered in oil cook for 8 minutes. Allow salmon to cool to room temp.

Mix together 1 cup extra virgin olive oil, 2 tablespoons of salmon caviar, 3 teaspoons finely chopped chives.

Mash 2 peeled avocados, 3 tomatoes, peeled and de seeded, 1 Spanish onion, diced and blended, 2 tablespoons lime juice, 6 drops of tabasco sauce, sea salt and freshly ground pepper and 3 tablespoons finely chopped chives.

To serve: Place avocado mixture in a small square mound in centre of each plate. Cut Salmon into 4 pieces and place on avocado mound (draining oil). Drizzle caviar dressing around plate and garnish with chive batons. Serves 4,

OLIVE OIL POACHED SALMON, CAVIAR DRESSING AND AVOCADO SALSA

Thursday Island

A gun emplacement erected for protection from the perceived threat from Russia in the nineteenth century still guards the northern approaches

of a small settlement. The early morning saw us nosing up the Albany Passage, a narrow stretch of water between Albany Island and Cape York. Again the beauty of our surrounds concealed a bitter past. Off shore lies the wreck of the 'Quetta' lost with 133 lives and in a pretty palm fringed cove the rainforest has reclaimed the tragic settlement of Somerset, once destined to be the hub of the north and once the seat of the Jardine family. It is only a short hop to Cape York and the sun had not risen above the thin cloud on the horizon before we were off the Cape protected by its two off lying islands – York and Eborac. A group of boats lay anchored off a wide tidal beach in the protected waters to the west of the point. Two hours later we were sheltered in the enclosed waters of the Ellis Channel. To starboard lay Thursday Island surrounded by its ring of protecting islands. We had reached our journey's end, a journey we have been blessed in being able to make. We hope that in some small measure we have captured the coast's exquisite beauty and that you too have enjoyed the journey.

Rob and Rosemary Peterswald. Hobart , Tasmania

recipes

The Photography

All photography by Rob & Rosemary Peterswald, except below:

Richard Bennett	Pages 6, 22, 34
Brett Boardman	Pages 14, 15, 21
Ray Cash	Page 142
Ben Cropp	Pages 191, 193
Camille Flores	Page 208
Fran Flynn	Pages 1, 130, 131, 136, 137
Jo Gamvros	Pages 148, 153, 169
Craig Lamotte	Pages 188, 198
Lizard Island	Pages 244, 245
Steven Nowakowski	Pages 207, 229
Nick Osborne	Pages 11, 13, 119, 217

food wine sun

journeys shore

endings shoreli

water sailing ea

food wine sun

journeys shore

endings shoreli

water sailing ea